MY YEAR
WITH A HORSE

HAZEL SOUTHAM

LION

D0318839

Published by Lion Books
an imprint of
Lion Hudson plc
Wilkinson House, Jordan Hill Road,
Oxford OX2 8DR, England
www.lionhudson.com/lion

ISBN 978 0 7459 6849 0
e-ISBN 978 0 7459 6850 6

First edition 2016

A catalogue record for this book is available from the British Library

Printed and bound in the UK, May 2016, LH26

For Duke, with heartfelt thanks

Contents

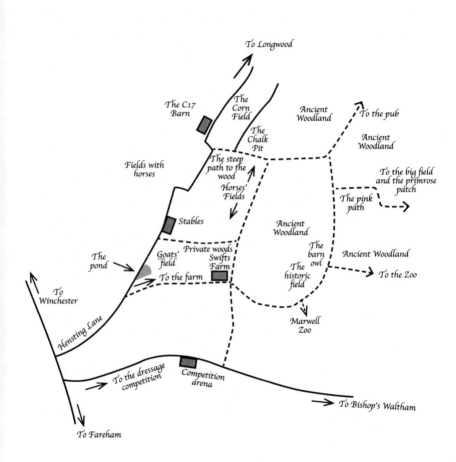

Acknowledgments

There are many people to thank, of course. Although he can't read, Duke gets the biggest thanks. He's not a famous horse that wins expensive races or international competitions. You won't see him on the front of a magazine. He's not a household name – although once, when I rang to pitch a news story to a chum at *The Daily Telegraph*, he said, "Hi Hazel; how's Duke?" So you can infer from that episode that either I talk about Duke too much, or the man at *The Telegraph* is very kind. Or both. Duke's not the most handsome horse you'll ever meet, I'm told, though clearly I would disagree with this. Duke transformed my life and I will be forever grateful to him. I hope he knows he is loved.

My thanks also go to Flick Homden and Tracey Wells, who at the time this all happened were instructors at the Hampshire Riding Therapy Centre. Their encouragement got me onto Duke's back in the first place, and kept me there. Some of the happiest moments of my life have been spent hacking round the woods near the stables with Flick. And thanks to the whole team at the riding centre for their patience, encouragement, and cheeriness.

I would also like to thank my horse-riding pals and their mounts: Anne-Marie Underwood (Lady), Debbie Gallagher (Jack), Jo Cook (Hippo), Kirsten Philpott (Blue Eyes), Kirsty Hobson (Spider), Paula and Alan Coleman (Chocci and Spike), and Michelle Cross (Rab). They've been tremendous company and very patient.

Thanks are also due to my other dear friends who have had to put up with stories of horse riding, when they couldn't care less about anything equine. They must have thought their old non-horsey friend had been kidnapped and a lookalike put in her place. You know who you are. Thank you. Chief among this group is Clare Kendall, my friend and photographer colleague. As we fly round the world together reporting on who-knows-what, she bears the brunt of most of the stories and can't escape, because, on a plane, you truly are a captive audience. Thanks for listening, Clare.

My final thanks go to my good friend Phil Comer for his support in this mad caper, despite his medical experience telling him that horse riding was A Very Bad Idea; and to my mother, Mary Southam, for not only letting me write this book but encouraging me all the way. Thank you both. Two finer people it is hard to imagine.

Professional and undying thanks go to the team at Lion Hudson, particularly my editor, Ali Hull. She was like a dog with a bone once she'd heard the idea for this book, and simply insisted that I write it, and kept on insisting until I did.

Thanks also to you, for reading this far. I hope you enjoy this book, and that it gives you some laughs along the way. But if you too are having a tough year, I trust that it gives you some hope for light at the end of a very long tunnel. It will come. The year is made up of seasons, and so is life.

Prologue

I didn't expect to have my life changed by a horse. I was scared of horses and, consequently, wanted nothing to do with them. But, following a New Year's resolution to overcome that fear, I ended up renting a big, trustworthy, middle-aged horse called Duke. He'd spent his life giving rides and joy to disabled adults and children at the Hampshire Riding Therapy Centre just outside Winchester. So he was just what I was looking for (although I didn't know that I was looking for it): reassuring, steady, and reliable. At first, I wasn't what he was looking for at all, as my nerves jangled and my confidence lagged. But in the end, over five happy years, I like to think that I became what he was looking for too: someone who loved and cared about him, tended to his needs, bought him warm rugs and tasty carrots, took him out for delightful rides in the woods, and didn't mind how much grass he ate when he was meant to be doing something else.

Our mini-adventures through Hampshire's ancient woodlands became, strangely, the highlight of my week. So, in one sense, this is a book written in profound thankfulness to Duke. But it is also the story of a year: of how making a decision to reach out beyond fear led, slowly and incrementally, to happiness, peace, and comfort. We Britons love animals, so if you've ever stroked a cat or patted a dog and felt better afterwards, you'll know what this feels like.

If you like horses, I hope you will enjoy this. But if you don't like them, don't worry. This is about far, far more than a horse. This is the story of a pivotal year in our family: as the Queen might say, our *annus horribilis*. Everyone has shockingly awful years, and this was one of ours. Remarkably, it was a horse that helped me through those twelve months. This was a surprise, as I was (I had thought) irredeemably frightened of horses. Above all else, this is a story of hope, because we can all sometimes feel that crying is the end of the story. But it isn't. All tears get wiped away in the end.

January

I open half an eye and groan. It is New Year's Day. All over Britain there are probably many people like me, who can barely lift their heads off their pillows. People who are regretting having that last glass of something really unpalatable – and possibly green – from the back of the drinks cabinet at 2 a.m.; something brought back from a family holiday in the Mediterranean that had never been touched. Now it has been and everyone is repenting of it.

The difference is that I haven't got a hangover. I simply can't face the year that lies ahead.

It was a bleak Christmas. Now, I appreciate that Christmas can be difficult for lots of people. There are arguably too many preconceptions of what it should be like and generally there's a great big gulf between those and reality. Magazines are full of decorative festive scenes in which, miraculously, time has been found to make beautiful displays for the table, the fireplace, the stairs, the hallway, and so on. In these pictures, the meal is never burned, the food all comes out of the oven at the same time, the Brussels sprouts actually look tasty and edible, and fresh-faced, smiling people in sparkling, fashionable clothes are having a jolly time. There are no rows, difficult relatives, or disappointing presents.

Helpful wall-planners give you a daily guide to things to do from about August onwards in order to be ready on time and have the opportunity and presence of mind to enjoy a relaxing glass of something bubbly with your family while the food magically cooks itself perfectly.

Of course, it's not like that in real life, is it? Despite this, I've always loved Christmas: decorating the tree, bringing in holly and ivy to make the house look festive, cooking up a storm, writing cards, wrapping gifts, being with loved ones, going to Midnight Mass at the cathedral and celebrating Jesus' birth.

It was all a joy. Then, six years before this story begins, my father – an intelligent, practical man – started to act strangely. He'd forget to do things. If he did them, he'd forget that he had done them. He got lost. He was unsure what he was saying.

He couldn't remember how to do basic tasks such as getting dressed, and he was achingly tired all the time. He slept for much of the day as well as the night.

Then he started to forget people and places; whole chunks of his life vanished from his memory. My mother and I knew, long, long before the diagnosis came, that it was dementia. Part of the cruel irony of dementia, however, is that often the sufferer doesn't understand what's happening to them or recognize the diagnosis as being true.

That was the case for my father. It was nonsensical, he said, that he should be considered "demented". He was perfectly fine, thank you. He'd always been intelligent, hadn't he? Was anyone questioning that now? Were we saying he was stupid? But time wore on and he wasn't fine.

By Christmas he was lost and scared, depressed by something he couldn't fathom and angry at a diagnosis that he utterly refuted. It was all too much for my mother, who first suffered with a dreadful cough and then got the norovirus. We'll gloss over the details. But I left her in bed and brought my father home with me. For three days I ran between the houses, cooking, cleaning, feeding, dressing, and washing both of them, administering medicine and sustenance. On Christmas Day, my father kept saying, "When do I give you my present?" I sat and wept, but that just annoyed him. "It's not my fault," he said, quite correctly.

"That doesn't stop it being sad," I replied. It didn't look at all like the pictures in magazines. There was no peace or goodwill among men this particular Christmas.

So I find myself on New Year's Day feeling that I have nothing to look forward to. Dementia is, after all, not something from which you miraculously recover. Whatever the road ahead holds, it can only be worse and more upsetting than what has gone before.

Yet, this year, I actually do have something to look forward to: a huge, middle-aged horse called Duke, who is to be my new best friend. The only snag is, as I have said, I am scared of horses. So just how have I got to this ridiculous point on a New Year's morning when events are at such a pass that the only thing I am looking forward to is something of which I am terrified?

It had begun with a resolution I'd made about eight Januarys before, to take up horse riding. Most of us make New Year's resolutions, but how many of us keep them? Plans to join the gym, lose weight, cut down on alcohol, quit smoking, all – it seems to me – go out of the window by mid-January. As I write this, I'm looking at a gym membership form and wondering how long I can put off filling it in.

Certainly I'd been uniformly rubbish at keeping New Year's resolutions in the past. Generally, I simply forgot that I'd made them and only remembered weeks or months later when someone asked me how I was getting on. Consequently, for years I'd given up making resolutions at all. What was the point if I couldn't even remember what I was meant to be quitting? It all seemed like such a negative start to the year ahead.

So I'd decided instead that I wanted a positive resolution that

I might actually keep, something that I would do, rather than not do. Realistically, I wasn't going to go to the gym. Clearly, that's still the case. Is there anything more boring? Mercifully, I didn't need to lose weight and I didn't smoke. So that left The Big Challenge: face a fear and overcome it. I was going to learn to ride.

Though I'd grown up in the countryside at a time when villages were still villages and not commuter belts, I'd never ridden. My childhood had been bucolic, an off-screen version of the popular 1970s TV series *The Good Life*. We grew all our own fruit and vegetables. I spent my summers picking soft fruit down the garden whilst listening to *Test Match Special* on an old radio that my father had cobbled together out of spare parts. We kept two dozen hens and a fearsome cockerel named Jock, of whom I was very scared. I walked, ran, cycled, and skipped everywhere and was outdoors from dawn until dusk. Even after dusk it was hard to keep me indoors. My mother invariably found me, in my nightclothes, sitting with my legs hanging outside the bedroom window, gazing into the gloaming, watching bats flit over the lawn, and drinking in the scent of lilac, clematis, and apple blossom.

I didn't set foot in a supermarket until I was sixteen years old and had never heard of McDonald's. It is hard to be more rural. Yet horses didn't come into the picture.

This was partly to do with class and money. Ordinary rural people like us didn't ride. Horses were, the unspoken message went, the preserve of the rich. And we were not rich. So somehow, somewhere along the line, a lack of familiarity with horses made me scared of them. I figured that, with the honourable exception of miniature Shetland ponies, they were all faster, bigger, and possibly more intelligent than I was. And even the miniature Shetlands might be faster. And more intelligent. I wasn't about to go anywhere near them. I didn't even watch horse racing on TV on principle.

There were, of course, other children who did have ponies. At primary school there was a small coterie of girls who would trot and gallop round the playground rather than walk or run. I despised them. Had they any idea how foolish they looked? Later, my best friend at grammar school owned her own pony. She kept trying to introduce me to him, with what I understand now as natural enthusiasm and a desire to share her love of horses. To my shame, I couldn't have been less interested. I'm still haunted by one afternoon spent at her house, when she asked me if I'd like to go and meet her pony, which was in a field nearby. "No thanks," I said, without even having the politeness to lie, visit the horse, smile and nod, and pretend to be interested. All these girls had far better manners than I did. They also knew a secret: horses are wonderful.

Winston Churchill once said, "There is something about the outside of a horse that is good for the inside of a man." But in those far-off growing-up days, the outside of a horse was not for me, or for most people I knew. In fact, the first time I saw someone riding around the village was when I returned, thirty years later, for a big family celebration. The sight of a woman riding a horse down the road that I'd grown up on took my breath away. I wanted to run up to her and say, "You do realize that no one rides here, don't you? This is a fast road these days. Children don't play in it any more. You're not safe. The countryside isn't what you think it is."

And then I realized that the fact that she *was* riding down my old road showed just how much the village had changed. Money had come in. People were living there not because they'd done so for generations, working the land, as my family had done, but because it meant they could get their children into good schools and it was only an hour from London. The countryside wasn't what I thought it was any more, either.

So how did the New Year's resolution come about? The answer is that I have a dreadful habit of looking things that terrify me in the eye and taking them on. It started at primary school. I had to be the first to put my hand up to volunteer or answer a question, just to get over the fear of saying anything in front of the class. Then I could relax and enjoy the rest of the lesson. Later on, this same personality trait meant saying "yes" to reporting assignments that I really wanted to say "no" to. When someone rang me up and offered to take me to my first war zone, I instantly said "yes". To do otherwise would have left me wondering what it would have been like for the rest of my life, and feeling like a coward. So I always tried to cover my innate fearfulness by looking adventurous. It was a very thin disguise.

More than twenty years later, however, I'm still hopping on planes and "going to places where things go bang", as my best friend Phil puts it. Choosing to overcome my fear of horses fitted a pattern. "Feel the fear and do it anyway," as the T-shirts say. However, it's safe to report that, when I had tried it, I had not fallen in love with horse riding. In fact, I was terrified. What was I doing on top of this horse? The answer was mostly panicking, sweating, hyperventilating, and wanting to get off quickly. Not surprisingly, it didn't go well. Patient – and not-so-patient – instructors tried to teach me. But all the time I was thinking, "I'm going to die. I'm going to die. Get me off this horse."

This was not helped, as you can imagine, by a horse wanting to oblige in that regard and running off with me onto the road, as well as the occasional fall. Horses know when you're scared. They can feel your fear. And, as flight animals, they are highly attuned to fear. So being scared only makes riding worse. The horse thinks, "What is this human scared of? Perhaps I ought to be scared too…" They freeze. You freeze. "What is the horse scared of?" you wonder, not realizing that it's you. Your life flashes before you. So does the horse's. It gets worse and results in the aforementioned bolting and decking of idiot girl on the ground. My riding experience had been very much more off than on, in every sense.

But, despite this, I loved being outdoors. I wanted to get back into the beech woods that dot the area where I live. This is because, when not picking fruit or running around the garden, my childhood had been spent in the beech woods that lay at the end of the road, as had those of every generation of my family before me. They were in my soul, or perhaps it was simply that my soul came alive in them. I certainly felt more at peace in the woods than anywhere else. I loved the drama of the dells, the majesty of the smooth tall beech trunks that seemed to reach up to the sky like a natural cathedral, the quietness, and, of course, the bluebells in spring.

Every season was a delight. Winter brought the chance to forage for kindling for the fire, and ivy to decorate the house at Christmas. Spring gave one of nature's greatest delights, the translucent unfolding leaves of the beech tree. In summer, the woods proved to be a cool place to play in the shade out of the heat of the day. And in autumn they were a riot of gold, yellow, and copper.

Yet, as an adult woman alone, I didn't fancy walking in the woods. What dark dangers lurked there? What strange men haunted the paths? Would someone with a machete leap out and attack me? Most probably not in leafy Hampshire, but I was never one to let the facts get in the way of a decent fear. "Why be calm when you can worry?" has always seemed to be my mantra. I figured, however, that a horse could outrun any trouble, so learning to ride would open up the woods for me once again. I was grittily determined not to be beaten by the terrors that horses presented.

Finally, when every sane person would have admitted defeat and taken up tennis, I met Duke. He's an Irish Draught horse: the equivalent of a tractor. And once, before the two World Wars, he would have done all the work on a farm, as well as taking the family to church on Sunday. Like a tractor, he is enormous.

He's 16.2 hands tall, which is so big that I can't see over even the lowest part of his back. He weighs three-quarters of a tonne, or 118 stone. I am 5'2" and weigh around 8 stone. So he is nearly fifteen times my weight. Seemingly, we were not well matched, though we were both in our middle years. He was fourteen at this point (which apparently is the equivalent of forty-five in human years) and I was forty-six. So we had that in common. The other thing we had in common was that, perhaps because of our age, neither of us wanted to go fast any longer.

"You *are* joking," I said to Flick, my riding instructor, the first time she brought him out into the stable yard for me to ride. "He's enormous."

"Don't worry," she said. "He's a gentle giant. You'll have no problems."

Actually, simply getting on Duke was a problem. Putting my foot into the stirrup from the ground (the first stage of getting on a horse) would involve raising my left foot to the level of my left ear while still staying upright. Then I'd need to propel myself with my right foot several feet into the air, so that I could leap up into the saddle.

Leap? Not a chance. My supple days were a hazy memory. I'd need a long run-up and a trampoline. No trampoline was available. But there was a three-foot-high ramp for disabled riders to use to get from their wheelchairs to the horse. I swallowed my pride, accepted what I was – middle-aged, stiff-jointed, and not a natural rider – and opted for the ramp as the only possible means of getting onto Duke's back.

In all other respects, though, Flick's summary of Duke proved to be right. He went about his work steadily. He was so tall that – once on board – I could peer into people's gardens and homes as we rode by. That was a definite plus point for someone with inbuilt curiosity, or, you could say, nosiness. But he was also kind, patient, and reliable. This was not a horse that was about to throw me off and run for home, however stupid, fearful, or hesitant I was. Slowly, I started to relax.

Some 3.5 million people ride horses in the UK, more than attend Premier League football matches each week. I began to think that I was one of them. But, in fact, all I was doing was turning up a couple of times each week, sitting on the horse, and doing what I was bidden as best I could by my instructors, Tracey and Flick.

This is not the same thing as riding at all. This is treating a horse like a sofa on legs. But I'd only learn the difference later.

I spent a fortune on lessons and enjoyed the security of being in the outdoor arena, a fenced-off area of sand where you and your horse can practise your moves. I spent another small fortune on riding out round the woods with either Flick or Tracey. Every Friday morning without fail, we'd be out there and the woods were reclaimed.

It had been on one of these rides the previous autumn, before our story starts, that the idea of committing myself to Duke was born. At Hampshire Riding Therapy Centre, it was possible to loan or rent a horse. You paid for a certain number of hours every week and could then do what you wanted. It was cheaper by far than owning a horse, and, as it turned out, cheaper than paying for weekly lessons and accompanied hacks round the woods. It was also a foreign land of responsibility and involvement about which I knew next to nothing.

"You should consider having Duke on loan," said Tracey, as we sauntered down the lane back from another successful walk round the woods. There are some moments in life when all the lights go on in your head, aren't there? Moments when you meet your life partner, find a job for which you're a perfect fit, walk into your future home and feel as if you already live there, or hear some great truth that speaks straight to your soul. This was one of those moments. I felt as if someone had whacked me hard round the head. Simultaneously, there seemed to be a large neon sign in the sky reading, "Don't miss this chance, Hazel."

"Er, really… why?" I asked, hesitantly. Loaning Duke seemed daunting. Was I really up to the task?

"Because it would be lovely for Duke," Tracey said.

I was puzzled. Wasn't she meant to be selling this to me on the basis that it would improve my riding? If I loaned Duke, she should be saying, I'd magically metamorphose into a proper horsewoman, gaining life skills along the way.

"No," Tracey said, dismissively. "Everyone needs to be loved and it would be nice for Duke to be loved by one person."

The idea had run through my brain like water down the cracks in limestone over the subsequent days and weeks. But Tracey had, as usual, said just the right thing. I am a hopeless animal lover. I've rescued cats, fed stray dogs, prayed for an injured chicken, and even sat with a rat while it died so that it didn't do so alone. If Duke needed someone to love him on a one-to-one basis, then I would be that person. From 1 January. And now it was 1 January, and the consequences of my decision were becoming real.

So I drag myself out of bed and head for the yard. I am set to ride with my new riding buddy, Annie. She has also decided to lease a horse that is, if anything, more enormous than Duke. Lady is a 17.1 hand shire horse who is also fourteen years old. Annie had fallen in love with her over the summer and had signed on the dotted line of the loan agreement at the same time as me.

Unlike me, however, Annie is a calm, confident, positive person. In her head, everything turns out well. In my head, life is fraught with dangers and terrible possibilities. What if the horse bolts? What if he is scared of something? What do I do if there's a tractor filling the road? What if Duke realizes that I haven't a clue what I'm doing?

So Annie is a good person to ride with this first day. She oozes positivity. It is a cold, crisp morning and the rest of the world is still in bed, or so it seems. We are the only mad fools willing or able to get out of bed on New Year's Day while there is nothing much abroad.

We tack up our horses. That's such a simple sentence to write. But on this first morning it is not a simple thing to do. I've never done it before. Arriving for a lesson meant I'd had the luxury of the horse already being prepared for me. I just had to get on with as little comic effect as possible.

Arriving for my first loan time means finding the right tack and putting it on, having first groomed my loan horse. Duke's saddle is, I feel sure, bigger than I am. I stagger under its weight and then attempt the manoeuvre of putting it on his back. I stagger some more. This is weightlifting, not horse riding.

And where exactly am I meant to put it? There is a lot of back on this horse, after all. Which is the right place? I fret that the saddle is too far forward, too far back. Annie has a cup of tea. Duke falls asleep. Time passes. Slowly.

Then there is the bridle. How do you put that on? How are you supposed to persuade a dozing horse to wake up, open his mouth, and accept a piece of metal attached to some leather straps? Not easily is the answer, if the horse knows, as Duke assuredly does, that I am a hopeless novice.

To enable us to get out of the yard before nightfall, Annie shows me how to put the reins over Duke's head and gently ease the bit into his mouth. Then there is the business of how to do up all the straps. There are plenty of them. Where do they all go? How tight should they be? Have I got it right? Is there anything, anything else at all, that I could worry about?

Yes there is. Is my riding hat on right? Have I got my mobile phone in case of a much-expected emergency? Is it turned to silent in order not to spook the horse if it rings? Are we about to die? Potentially only of boredom, in Annie's case.

Finally, I get on board and we head out onto the winding lane that leads to the woods. But wait. I've forgotten something. There is definitely something missing. I know what it is: it's the riding instructor. Help.

Riding without an instructor for the first time is akin to having the stabilizers taken off your bike when you're a child. But what is worse is that I am on a large, independent-minded animal, not a bike, and there is no one holding on to the back saying "You can do it" and pushing. The horror. Now I know I really am going to die on this road on New Year's Day.

Instead of dying, however, we plod steadily onwards: two women on their majestic, giant horses. It is a timeless image, if you discount our hi-visibility jackets and hard hats. Up the lane we walk, meeting a few other riders out for a New Year's Day freshener, a dog walker, and a couple of cars. Duke takes it all in his lengthy stride: ears pricked, exhaling loudly in a sound that I will come to know is the equivalent of a human's sigh of relaxation. "Ahhh, bliss," he is saying. He hasn't been out partying as far as we know and is on a mission to get to the woods. We have to keep stopping and waiting for Lady, who possibly has been on the equine sherbets.

Then we head round the woods, our generic term for the acres of ancient woodland that stretch behind the stables up to Marwell Zoo and beyond. Moreland's Copse, Cowleaze Copse, West Copse, and Horsham Copse are mainly made up of beech, ash, and oak trees, with an understorey of hazel, hawthorn, blackthorn, and field maple. And they are really, really old. Cowleaze Copse was once part of a medieval deer park that was in existence from the thirteenth century. There are ancient monuments, veteran trees, tracks that were main roads 800 years ago and more. Both Roman and Celtic remains have been found here. Indeed, the seemingly innocuous point at which we turn into the woods used to be a Celtic settlement. It is a place that lives and breathes history. A network of bridleways and footpaths links these four copses and Longwood, which lies several miles away, and therefore is as yet off my radar. But this largely hidden network allows us to get off the road and go at our own pace. Today, that pace is fairly slow, despite Duke's enthusiasm.

Some 120 acres of this woodland belong to Marwell Zoo. There are records of a settlement here dating back to Saxon times. Marwell gets a mention in the Domesday Book. And by the eleventh century the Bishop of Winchester had established a college of priests on the site with some 2,000 acres of woodland, which makes the area we ride through feel very small indeed, though we view it as being extensive.

Over the centuries, these very woods have provided timber to help build Marwell Hall (one of the homes of the Seymour family and thus, the rumours go, visited by Henry VIII when out courting Jane Seymour) and Winchester Cathedral. Beech, oak, ash, and cherry were all grown for timber.

Today, much of the woodland is still managed. The hazel

stands are coppiced on a seven-year rotation. This lets the light in, allowing rare plants such as the early purple orchid, the pyramidal orchid, and the common spotted orchid to thrive here. It also provides stacks of timber that are habitats for invertebrates. As I am the owner of both an open fire and a wood-burning stove, these woodpiles give me "wood envy". I wish, very much, that they were mine.

I've always loved woodland in winter. There is a stark beauty to its stillness on days like today. Everything seems frozen, frosted, and dead. The ground is carpeted in brown beech leaves. A thin winter light filters through the tracery of the branches. In its simplicity it seems to me to be even lovelier than the woods in summer. And there is silence. Once we are into the woods, with their arching branches, stacks of coppiced hazel branches, the occasional yew or holly tree, and clumps of butcher's broom, we see no one.

We are followed round our circular route by a series of robins that hop from tree to tree to the edge of their territory, and then pass us on to the next robin. It brings new meaning to the phrase "a round robin". But it also shows how much more you notice in nature when you go slowly enough. You really appreciate the countryside from the back of a horse.

For forty-five minutes I am thinking only about what I'm doing: riding Duke sufficiently well to get home in one piece; the utter relaxation of drinking in the woods from the back of a horse; chatting easily with Annie about anything and nothing.

The stress of two very ill parents and the worry about their future have simply fallen away. I find I am not gritting my teeth or frowning any longer, which I am perpetually doing otherwise. Surely horse riding should be available on the NHS for stressed relatives like me? It is better than therapy.

Being the carer for someone with dementia is like falling very slowly, silently, down a deep, dark wormhole that has no end. You are screaming and falling, but no one knows that you're there. No one hears you cry. You are utterly alone and you fear the inevitable end almost more than the fall.

In 2015, there were said to be some 850,000 people in the UK living with dementia. That number is going up all the time. By 2025, there will be 1 million. One in six people aged over eighty have dementia and some 60,000 deaths a year are directly attributable to it. The financial cost of dementia in the UK is estimated at £26 billion per year, according to the Alzheimer's Society. This is almost as much as the government spends on transport. But there's a hidden cost too; it's the cost to those around the person who – like my father – has dementia.

Three-quarters of doctors say that their dementia patients have to rely on family, friends, and unpaid carers because they receive insufficient help from health and social care services, which are, as the recession continues, strapped for cash.

How you cope with dementia is thus coming down to how much money you have in the bank. If you have a sizeable sum, you may be in the fortunate position of being able to buy in care whilst your parents remain at home. If you haven't, then you are in a postcode lottery. If your local council has managed to hold on to its social care services, then you may just manage.

But government cuts over successive years have made it hard for social care provision to be maintained, and worse is to come, with the government postponing its plans to limit the amount of money you have to pay towards your care (£72,000). Essentially, the take-away message is: if you're old and get dementia, your family will have to sell your home in order to care for you. What kind of a society is that?

This is the stuff that rolls round my head every night and stops me sleeping. I know we're not coping with my father's dementia, but what are the alternatives? Kind people come from the local council and advise us on the options: day care one day a week seems to be the first step. This will provide respite for my mother from the constant anxiety of wondering whether my father's injured himself, fallen, or wandered off and the endless, endless questions that he asks, simply to reassure himself that the world is as he thinks it is. Which it isn't.

I am an only child. I love my parents. I want to do my level best to help them. I'm lucky, as I live only a few miles away from them. So I call in several times a week; I try to sort out new levels of care, when possible; mostly I listen to my mother and try to prop her up. But I am conscious that my best is not enough. To mix my metaphors, I feel like Mickey Mouse in "The Sorcerer's Apprentice" sequence in Disney's *Fantasia*, running faster and faster to fill buckets of water and not being able to keep up with the manic magic that surrounds him.

Only this isn't funny.

It feels as if I can't do anything properly. I currently work as a journalist half the week for The British and Foreign Bible Society and fall on that time like a person reaching an oasis in a desert. The joy of working as a respite from caring is unbounded. But always in the background is the worry about how my parents are coping, and I know I get distracted from my work.

For the other half of the week I am a jobbing hack for national newspapers and magazines, finding stories and selling them to news and features editors. But the recession means that newspapers' budgets are tighter. Fewer stories are being bought in. Plus my attention is taken by the daily anxieties and stresses of my father's condition, so I'm not going out hunting for stories, as a good journalist should. And because I am working, or at least trying to, I'm not spending the time with my parents that they really need.

I crawl into bed at night thanking God that we've got through another day, but fearing the next one. The spectre of the future hangs over me at every moment. I worry about what care both my parents will need and how that can possibly be afforded. I rage silently against politicians who think it's all right that what they always refer to as a "hard-working family" should be required, when old, ill, and infirm, to sell their home in order to pay for their care; that this may be what befalls my family. Why should the government inherit my parents' house, not me? I'd like the Prime Minister to come and explain it to me, and I could explain to him, very succinctly, why this is daylight robbery and that consequently I believe him and the Chancellor of the Exchequer to be little better than highwaymen.

And what happens if, in years to come, I get dementia – I who live alone? There's hardly a minute of any day in which I am not entirely taken up by these potential situations and my seeming inability to do anything about them. Except these particular forty-five minutes, riding Duke round the woods with Annie and Lady, when I feel as if I have entered another world where these stresses do not exist. A light bulb goes on in my head. This is why people ride horses! I am hooked and I know it. My bank manager – if he could see me right now – would weep. My bank account is about to haemorrhage money. But there is now a light at the end of my long, deep wormhole, and it takes the shape of a big, steady, middle-aged horse called Duke.

February

Hensting Lane, where the stables are, is a little bit of rural heaven. Even people who've lived in Hampshire for many years don't know that it exists. Some may have heard of the pub at the end of the road, as those of us whose navigation skills predate satnav can still find their way around the countryside using pubs and churches as landmarks. But few have been down there. In fact, it's probably safe to say that you don't go down Hensting Lane unless you live there, or are a horse rider, a cyclist, a delivery driver, or a farmer. It is not a road to anywhere. But, for me, Hensting Lane has become my happy place, because it is where Duke lives.

It's a narrow lane that runs for a couple of miles through cornfields and farms of goats, alpacas, and Jersey cows. There is a vast pond, home to moorhens and coots that scuttle across the road and to frogs and toads, which have to be protected from cars in the spring mating season. The toads live in the woodland that tops the field opposite, but, problematically, on the other side of the road from the pond. The common toad, whose Latin name (*Bufo bufo*) is tremendous, spends its life in the leaf litter of woods. But it migrates to the pond where it was born in order to mate. This all works excellently until a road is built. Then carnage ensues as drivers unwittingly flatten the toads who are heading out to mate.

So, in Hensting Lane, locals have set up an annual Toad Watch to assist the toads in reaching their destination. On damp spring evenings, people wearing hi-vis jackets patrol the road with buckets, scooping up toads and depositing them on the other side of the road, by the pond. Sometimes the toads don't want to be helped. The males are used to hitching a ride with the (much larger) females with whom they will then hope to mate on arrival at the pond. The best place to spot a female is, apparently, the middle of the road, so rescued male toads often head back to the road to check out the passing totty. As this can be very life-limiting indeed, the local Toads & Roads Patrol keep scooping them up until the small hours and repeat the process every damp night, thus saving many hundreds of toady lives.

The hedgerows are home to plenty of sparrows. Pea-brained pheasants and red-legged partridge (which if anything are even more stupid) run about in the lane. Pigeons (or, as any horse will tell you, huge, menacing, sabre-toothed pigeons) fly up as we ride by. Occasionally we see buzzards, kestrels, and red kites circling overhead.

It is easy to mark the changing seasons in Hensting Lane. Winter often brings floods. The lane lies in a narrow valley, and water both runs down the clay-and-chalk hills and rises up from the stream that flows along the edge of the road. The two combine, resulting sometimes in large, extended puddles with their own duck populations and some years in floodwaters that prevent any vehicular access and go over the top of your wellington boots for good measure. The spring brings exuberance and an abating of the waters. The hedgerows froth with cow parsley, both white and red May blossom, and the laciness of elderflowers. In summer, the cottage gardens that dot the lane burst into colour, bedecked with roses, jasmine, and wisteria. A line of poplar trees shivers even on the hottest, stillest of days. By the autumn, the woods around the lane are revealing themselves in every colour of seasonal glory. And there are sloes to be picked for the annual batch of sloe gin. In several places, the trees arch over the road, forming a tunnel that is dark even in summer months.

It is, in short, a piece of English countryside that has defied time and change, though now, even here, wealthier homeowners are moving in and the size of the houses along the lane is increasing. But, while it may be rural, the lane still has traffic. There are seven riding establishments along the road, whether they be homes with horses, livery yards, or, like ours, a public stables offering lessons. This means that many of the drivers and cyclists who go along the lane are used to horses and allow for all eventualities. But not all of them. There are some who cannot, it seems, tell the difference between a horse and a bollard, and expect the former to behave the same as the latter. Some pass by so close when you are riding that you could reach out and touch not just the car but the people inside it. Sometimes you feel like doing so, and not in a friendly spirit either. So I must be prepared for anything that may come along the lane and learn to protect Duke and myself from road-going danger. I sign up for a course to teach me properly, officially, how to ride on the road.

Phil's medical training gives him a dim view of my horse-riding ambitions. He won't tell me, but I imagine that he's seen too many people arrive at A&E with life-changing injuries, having fallen from a horse. He doesn't want me to become one of them. He doesn't say so, but I am sure that he would much, much rather that I returned to the relative safety of aerobics classes, where the worst I'm likely to do is pull a muscle. When pushed, all he'll say is, "Horse riding is about as safe as being strapped to the side of a speeding, unmanned motorbike."

The statistics bear out his concerns. The British Horse Society reports that there are around 3,000 accidents every year involving horses, and that about half of them occur on minor roads, such as Hensting Lane. This year alone the police will record some 133 horse-riding casualties nationwide. There will be two serious injuries to children out riding, and four adults will die.

So, in a bid to avoid becoming one of their number, and to ensure that my chances of survival are better than that of some of the dimmer-witted toads, I undertake the Riding and Road Safety Test, along with 4,000 others across the UK. Because part of the test involves dismounting and remounting your horse, I do this on a small pony called Leroy, as there is a very good chance that I can manage this with him and only a smidgeon of a hope with Duke.

A gang of us meet at the yard once a week after work. We go through the basics: riding straight along the road (you must look over your shoulder to check for traffic behind you every three seconds); turning right and left; waiting at junctions; and passing parked cars. We learn the appropriate hand signals – and no rudeness here, please – for turning right and left, and asking a driver to slow down or stop.

Then we come to the real joker in the pack: going round a roundabout. In case you ever need to do this, let me explain. You approach the roundabout looking all around for traffic, glancing over your shoulder every three seconds as well as watching out for oncoming vehicles, then you indicate right (assuming you're not instantly turning left). You look over your shoulder and repeat the arm signal. You look over your shoulder again.

Then, when it is safe to do so, you get onto the roundabout, staying on the nearside, paying particular attention to traffic turning left in case it decides to drive right through you.

You keep indicating right and looking behind you every three seconds, whilst going forward on an animal that has a mind of its own, holding the reins in one hand and manoeuvring round the roundabout with all its traffic. Finally, when you reach your exit (after what may seem to be an entire lifetime) you indicate left, still doing all the looking-behind-you-repeatedly stuff.

"You are advised", the handbook says, "to avoid using roundabouts." You don't say. Anyway, for the purposes of the test we must show that we can do this. So we practise and practise with a pretend roundabout made of traffic cones in the outdoor arena under floodlights in the evenings. We do this in pouring rain, in biting winds, in bitter cold, and I learn that no weather is so biblically awful as to allow a horse rider the excuse of staying indoors. These are hard-bitten types that laugh in the face of all weather, except perhaps thunderstorms, of which many horses (including the seemingly unflappable Duke) are scared.

We read our *Highway Code*, as there is a written test too. "When did you last read yours?" is the question on the back of *The Highway Code*. For me the answer is about thirty years ago, and frankly I can't remember what all the signs are, or even having seen some of them before. I sit up in bed each night trying to memorize them.

There are more horror stories about why it's important that I learn this. "Every day, on average, around nine people are killed and around eighty are seriously injured in road collisions," says *The Highway Code*. "So it is as important as ever that all road users, including drivers, motorcyclists, cyclists, horse riders and pedestrians, should update their knowledge of *The Highway Code*."

The test guides to a car's braking distance make this all far, far worse. If a driver is travelling at 30 mph it will take them 30 feet to think about stopping, once they have seen you and your horse, and another 45 feet to do so. That's 75 feet, which is a long way. If they don't spot you immediately, because they are sneezing, dozing, changing their music, chatting, just not concentrating or, perish the thought, on their mobile phone, it will take longer. If they're going at 50 mph (and let's just say that not everyone takes Hensting Lane at a steady 30) it'll take 175 feet for a car to stop. No one actually says that you haven't a chance of surviving this, and neither does the horse, and possibly not the driver. They don't have to.

But the British Horse Society claims that if you're wearing high-visibility clothing whilst riding, you give the driver an extra three seconds to see you. That could make all the difference between life and death.

I buy a high-vis jacket in the manner of a medieval Christian buying a relic to protect them from harm. In the same spirit, I buy Duke a high-vis exercise-sheet that he will wear when we are out on wet days. It's seven feet long, runs from the top of his tail to the base of his neck, keeps off the rain, and is so bright that quite possibly it can be seen from Mars. He looks like a police horse in it. No one, no matter how inattentive, can miss us now, I think to myself.

Despite my high-vis relics, the stats are quite enough to make you never head out onto the roads at all. But if the woods are to be ridden in, then a short amount of riding on the road must be undertaken. It is a means to an end. And, as the saying goes, knowledge is power. If I know what to do on the road, I will be safer, Duke will be safer, and everyone around me (including car drivers) will be safer too.

The day of the test dawns bright and clear. I am petrified. After our written test, we lead our mounts up to one of the top fields behind the stables where an assault course has been laid out. This includes a parked car. We've done this perfectly well in the school when it's been a hay bale standing in for a car. But on the day, it's a real car and the winter sun is throwing a long shadow ahead of it. Leroy doesn't like the look of it at all and goes sideways several feet into what would be the road, could have been oncoming traffic, but was just a field. I worry that I've failed.

Then we are given individual tests up and down the lane to see how we handle reality. Instructors with clipboards dot the route watching us avoid manhole covers (they are slippery if you are wearing metal shoes, which of course Leroy is), a dog in a parked car, blind bends, and passing traffic, and then comes the moment when they tell us to dismount, walk on, and remount further along the lane.

My heart is in my mouth, but I'm thankful that there are no roundabouts to negotiate or hard-to-remember road signs.

Happily, we all pass and are now deemed sufficiently prepared to ride out alone on Hampshire's roads. I certainly feel well prepared and know what I should be doing in most circumstances, even if I don't always remember to do it.

With the safety box ticked, it is time to return to the beloved day job: getting on planes, rather than horses, and heading for interesting parts of the world. As my father's dementia has got worse, I've barred myself from taking holidays, on the grounds that I don't feel confident leaving my parents to fend for themselves; the stress is too great on my mother. But I haven't carried this over to foreign reporting assignments. Everyone needs a break, I reason with myself illogically, and if that break is two weeks of intense work in Ethiopia (as it is now) rather than a week on a Spanish beach, then so be it.

My Bible Society colleague, Rich, and I spend a fraught few days reporting on the African Biblical Leadership Initiative conference, a scheme set up by Bible Society to see biblical values discussed by politicians, civic society leaders, and churchmen, in the spheres of good governance (no one's openly calling it corruption), conflict, poverty, and reconciliation.

This wouldn't necessarily make the headlines, but in Tahrir Square in nearby Egypt, something appears to be happening. Both supporters and opponents of President Hosni Mubarak have taken to the streets. First, they are on foot. Then mounted riders and men on camels attack anti-government protestors. One man is killed. More than 400 are injured.

The Arab Spring has begun. Every night we are glued to the TV in the hotel bar that screens *Al-Jazeera* round the clock. There is violence, turmoil, and uncertainty. The conference we're reporting on speaks into that, and gets a few column inches in the African press, as well as back home. But going about our work is fraught with difficulty. My computer and phone both stop working. It turns out later that both have taken an instant dislike to Ethiopia's calendar. Here it is 2003, not 2011. My computer and phone know damn well that it is 2011 and give up the effort of trying to work in a parallel universe.

The parallel universe of Ethiopia's calendar is, for us, maddening, but also very interesting. In the UK, like most of the world, we work on the Gregorian calendar, invented by Pope Gregory XIII in 1582; though, if we're honest, Britain didn't take it up until 1752. The Ethiopians are having none of it, basing their calendar on a different interpretation of the annunciation of Christ (I kid you not). This means that their calendar has twelve months comprised of thirty days, plus a thirteenth month made up of five or six days. There is also a leap year every fourth year. So here we are back in 2003 without obvious use of a time machine.

Another hazard to communication with 2011 and the rest of the world is that there is an African Union Summit taking place in Addis Ababa simultaneously and we spend vast tracts of time at roadblocks as world leaders' convoys hold up traffic.

Much of the bandwidth (or internet access) is hijacked for the world leaders to use. So we are stuck with nothing. We can't file our stories or upload pictures or videos. We could do with a loft of carrier pigeons.

We are trapped in a daily cycle of frustrations and hopes. The task of sending our stories home (known as filing copy), which in the UK would take five minutes, takes five hours on average. So we join the rest of the international press corps at the Sheraton Hotel, the only place with its own guaranteed internet access. From here we can file. We just have to get there through all the roadblocks in order to be able to do it.

I've borrowed an Ethiopian computer and phone that inhabit the parallel universe of 2003, so I can finally communicate with the outside world, but every day is stressful. While I'm away, my mother marks her eighty-third birthday. I worry, given her state of health, that it will be her last and that I'll have missed it. But I manage to ring home and find that she loved the flowers I sent and had lots of visitors, gifts, cards, and phone calls, so is feeling and sounding cherished, which is a comfort.

The conference ends, and one of the senior executives declares a day off for the team. She insists that I accompany her to a local beauty parlour where relaxing massages are offered. I can't turn her down, but between you and me have never found massages relaxing. While I'm lying there I'm thinking of the list of things I should be doing. That makes me all the more stressed!

This time, through gritted teeth, I find myself thinking that I'd much, much rather be going horse riding. I've only had Duke on loan for a month, and already, despite my fears, spending time with him is the way that I'd choose to relax. I can't quite believe it.

The conference delegates fly home. Rich and I remain and are joined by video cameraman Ed and photographer Clare for a more general reporting assignment that will see us travelling outside Addis. Clare is an international photographer and a personal friend, so it's great to have her turn up. We visit people in their homes, spend a day at an orphanage (which is so caring and friendly that it's one of the happiest places you could wish to be), and hope to do some interviews in a prison. Then stubborn bureaucracy gets in the way and we are barred from the jail. The lads take the unexpected spare day to edit their footage. Clare and I take to the hills on a hunch that we might have spotted a story.

Mountains ring Addis Ababa. Ethiopia's distance runners train up here – among other places – running for hour after hour along the mountain roads. This is what altitude training looks like. No wonder Haile Gebrselassie, Kenenisa Bekele, and Tirunesh Dibaba are all athletic legends.

Also heading up the mountainside are women bent double under the weight of vast bundles of wood. We want to talk to them. So it is on the mountainside that we meet forty-five-year-old Cholbe Chotto. She has, thus far, walked the equivalent distance of going twice round the world, collecting wood, and she's still walking. She should be given a medal or a break, or both.

Cholbe is one of 30,000 women who collect and sell wood for fuel across Ethiopia. Half of them work, as she does, on the mountains that surround Addis Ababa. Ninety per cent of Ethiopia's fuel comes from wood. Locally, people buy it to cook the nation's staple dish of *injera*, a pancake-like dish. But this heavy reliance on wood has resulted in an environmental crisis in Ethiopia. In the last 100 years, the country's forests have been slashed from covering 35 per cent of the land to just 3 per cent in 2000.

The government is now trying to redress this by protecting the forests and instituting a tree-planting scheme. In the last decade Ethiopia's woodlands have started to grow back, now making up an estimated 9 per cent of the land.

So for Cholbe – and the thousands of women like her – there's a real problem. Their work is now illegal, and government guards protect the forests that they rely on for their living. But the demand for wood for fuel remains, and few other sources of work are available.

Cholbe lives in a small wooden hut in an illegal settlement – known as Cheffe – in the eucalyptus forests outside Addis Ababa. It's made up of forty-five tin-roofed dwellings, many of which have been there for thirty years. But today Cholbe and her neighbours live under constant threat of eviction. She's been collecting wood from the mountain for twenty-seven years, in the process walking barefoot the distance mentioned above.

As if this weren't gruelling enough, Cholbe is disabled. During the 1984 famine, she suffered a stroke after giving birth to twins, who died. She never regained the use of the right side of her body.

"It's very, very hard work," she says. "I've been collecting wood since 1984 and I've never seen any change in my life. I am only able to use one hand to collect the firewood. I use my teeth to tie the bundle sometimes. Because of my stroke, I fall down every day."

Before dawn, Cholbe and her neighbours head for the mountain. They walk between 10 and 15 km per day (6–9 miles) to gather wood and take it to market. By mid-afternoon they're heading home with their bundles, which can weigh up to 50 kg (8 stone), in many cases more than the women themselves. I want to experience what that feels like, but no one will let me hold their bundle of wood, even for a minute. It's too heavy for you, they say.

Three o'clock is rush hour on Entoto Mountain. Groups of women walk down bent double with their heavy loads, their feet flattened by years of carrying such weights. They are passed by small herds of donkeys carrying hay. Buses and cars take locals and visitors up to the ancient churches that draw tourists to the mountain.

Many of the women's eucalyptus bundles are at least six feet across. Because of her disability, Cholbe can't carry this much.

Instead, she collects wood in a sack, earning between 5 and 10 birr (20–40p) per day.

"Sometimes I fast because I don't have enough food," she says. "I sacrifice my stomach and I pay the rent because that's something serious. I may not eat lunch or breakfast because there's not enough money to live on."

Poverty isn't the only problem faced by these women. Wood carrying is also dangerous. The women we meet report that government guards who protect the forest bribe them to walk on the main road, beating them if they resist. They also report rape and even murder. The women are even at risk of attacks by groups of hyenas that live in the forest. Everyone knows someone who's been attacked, and some have friends who've been killed by the animals.

We talk to staff at a church at the foot of the mountain who are working with the women, running loan schemes for them to start small businesses in alternative trades. The staff also visit the sick, and provide food on feast days in the sure and certain knowledge that these families – who help other people to cook their food – don't have much to eat themselves.

It's all sobering stuff and certainly puts my own experiences into perspective.

After two weeks of this, which sees us all fall in love with Ethiopia, its peerless blue skies, dignified people, and dramatically beautiful scenery, we head home.

I find that I am looking forward to seeing not only my parents, and George, my large, affable Maine Coon cat, but also Duke. It's the first time in my life that I've looked forward to seeing a horse. The tectonic plates in my soul are shifting.

Jet lag overwhelms me. For a couple of weeks my body clock slowly adjusts itself to being back in the UK and 2011. I wake before dawn and am in bed embarrassingly early. In between times, not very much is going on in my brain. I am dog, dog, dog tired. I know that, even with my newly acquired road-riding skills, I am not safe on the roads, even in the quietness of Hensting Lane. It is, I feel quite sure, important to have your eyes open and your mind alert whilst trying to steer 750 kg of horse down a road. So, as this is far from being the case, I go to the yard and lean against Duke as if he were a wall. I'm so tired that I could, quite easily, stand there and fall asleep with my head on his warm, sweet-smelling neck.

Elsewhere, February is the month where some lucky people enjoy Valentine's Day with their loved ones, and the high street thanks its lucky stars that there's a big spending day in the calendar this soon after Christmas. In Britain we spend around £1.3 billion on gifts on Valentine's Day. Most of this, it would appear, is spent by panicking men.

According to a US survey, they have good reason to do so. In America, 53 per cent of women surveyed said that they would dump a boyfriend who didn't buy them a gift on Valentine's Day. Whilst the day doesn't rival Christmas, Easter, or Mothering Sunday for spending power, we are certainly shelling out a lot of cash in mid-February, when some of us are still paying off our Christmas credit-card bills. Some 65 per cent of Britons send Valentine's Day cards, not wishing to be dumped like their American cousins. A further 21 per cent send flowers. Twenty-six per cent go out for a meal. Five per cent buy jewellery. And 3 per cent take the very high-risk strategy of buying underwear.

As there isn't a whiff of romance in my life, I decide to join the fray nonetheless and buy something for my new love, Duke. Romantically, I buy him two winter-weight rugs from an online supplier, in the hope that they will keep him warm and dry out in the fields, as the rain and cold of late winter continue.

Somewhere in my addled brain, I trust that he will understand that the ensuing warmth comes from me, and that these two rugs will help us to bond.

I may be growing very fond of this middle-aged horse, but he's not warming to me quite as much, especially as I've been away for a fortnight. He is an intelligent creature and is used to the experienced staff at the yard. He knows, therefore, that I'm an idiot. Grooming, cleaning tack, and tacking him up remain daunting tasks.

For now, warm winter rugs in hand, I decide that jet lag forces me to keep two feet on the ground, and, rather than riding, we will concentrate instead on spending time together in the stable. I will groom Duke until he shines, and then I'll do it again.

With a horse the size of Duke, and in winter weather, this can take as long as you want it to. First you must hose the worst of the mud off your horse's legs, feet, and stomach. Then, so that he doesn't get cold, you should towel-dry his legs at least, and stomach if you can manage it. Then the brushing begins. First you get the remaining dried mud off places to which you have not taken the hose. You pick out his feet, thus ridding them of mud and stones. You spray his tail with an anti-tangle liquid and apply yourself to getting the knots out of it for an indeterminate amount of time. Then you brush, brush, and brush him again all over, wipe his eyes, and treat his legs and hooves with oil to protect them from the worst of the mud and wet. And when you sit down afterwards you discover that you have a very clean horse and are absolutely filthy yourself. No matter.

After you've fed and watered a horse, provided it with shelter, kept it re-shod every six weeks, attended to its medical needs, and groomed it until it shines, everything else is shopping. And I do love shopping. I particularly enjoy shopping for The Right Kit.

This dates back to being eleven years old and being presented with the shopping list of approved uniform and kit for grammar school. There was a summer uniform and a winter one. We were to wear short, pleated gym skirts for tennis and hockey, but athletics shorts for running. We were required to have navy socks with two light-blue bands for hockey, white socks for tennis and athletics. There was even a rule about the colour of underwear and the length of skirts. There were pencil cases, pencils, ink pens, erasers, and approved bags to be bought, along with an *Oxford English Dictionary* and a thesaurus.

I loved all of this and still revel in the idea of having the right kit for the right activity. Horse riding plays firmly into my shopping-for-kit weakness. So as well as the two rugs for Duke, which you could somehow justify on the grounds of animal welfare, I'd bought my own tack box and filled it with a range of brushes for all occasions: a soft one for the face, medium for the body, a horsey hairbrush for the tail, and a stiff brush for removing water and mud. There are scrapers for cleaning a horse after a shower, chalk for whitening his feathers at a show (feathers are the long bits of hair that hang down over some horses' hooves), lotions and potions for summer and winter. A horse's nose is pink and very tender, so it's important (yes, important) to buy some suntan lotion. In February.

Then you must have some shampoo for showering your horse, which you won't do in earnest until the far-off hot days of the summer for fear of freezing him to death. And baby wipes are also a good idea, to keep the corners of his eyes clean. As a horse depends on having strong hooves, invest, say Tracey and Flick, in the best-quality hoof oil you can afford. This protects the hoof from the weather and keeps it moist. Then you must buy a large container of pig oil, which you'll spray or wipe onto his legs to keep off the worst of the mud.

Thank goodness for bank savings accounts. I spill the contents of mine onto these purchases and the tack box itself. Whilst everyone calls it a box, many people actually have a bag. What I've spotted in the shops, though, is a box with a lid that doubles as a step. This, cunningly, gives me an extra foot of height. Suddenly, I can both see and reach Duke's back. Grooming no longer involves waving my arms about above my head in blind hope. I can see what I am doing. You'd think that would make a difference. It does for me, though I look like a small child standing on an orange box, adding to the ongoing comedy of my riding ability. For Duke the difference is marginal: I am still an idiot, just one standing on a box.

He has a condition called navicular in his front feet, which is rather like osteoporosis in people. Small bones are slowly crumbling, resulting in pain and on-and-off lameness. Right now, Duke's feet hurt. He lets me know this by refusing to allow me to pick out his feet. This is something you must do before and after you ride, to check for stones and other objects that might have got lodged in the horse's feet. You also need to do it morning and evening, as good practice.

Duke's feet are the size of dinner plates and a good deal heavier. All his 118-stone weight bears down on them and he refuses to let me pick them up, one after the other, to remove any stones. I lean against him with all my eight-stone weight, to try to force his leg up. He leans back with three-quarters of a tonne of weight and wins.

I sit on my box and think about it. Force clearly isn't the way forward. Gentleness might be. If my feet hurt I'd want whoever handled them to be very, very kind indeed. Gently and slowly, I ask him for a foot, starting at the back with the less painful ones. He lifts a limb. I pick his foot out and place it carefully back down again, telling him all the while what a good boy he is. We repeat this four times.

We look at each other. Gentleness and kindness, the old boy seems to be saying to me. Those are your ways forward, Hazel. Standing in the encircling gloom of a February day, wet, cold, and liberally covered in mud, hay, pig oil, and horse poo, I think that we may have turned a very small corner.

March

We are standing on the cusp of March, worrying. I'm worrying about whether I've got too much work, or not enough. The life of a journalist is always precarious and as I am self-employed for half of my week, this is particularly true for me. My father, if he could articulate it, would be worrying about what on earth is happening to him. This manifests itself in the normal things of life (dealing with banks, understanding debit cards, making phone calls, gardening) not making any sense at all. My mother – who is too polite to talk about her worries – is nevertheless overwhelmed by them. She almost vibrates with the stress of Daddy's dementia. Her blood pressure is sky-high.

Sleep eludes me. When it does come I have nightmares in which variously both my parents die; or my mother dies and I am unable to look after my father; or my father dies and I am unable to look after my mother. I wake repeatedly, drenched in sweat despite the cold weather.

Two months in, I'm learning that a solution to this endless worry is to spend time with Duke. I can forget myself in his day-to-day needs, and you do have to concentrate if you are steering three-quarters of a tonne of horse along a road.

So Duke and I mark the start of our third month together with our first ride out alone. This means no friends to rely on, and no instructors. All the support systems are turned off. It's a huge step forward into the unknown.

Accordingly, we don't gallop off into the next county, which we would do if this were a film. Instead, in real life, we take a gentle stroll down Hensting Lane. Though I am wrapped up against the bitter cold of a late winter day, I feel naked. Riding alone, even for such a short distance, makes me feel exposed. It really is just the horse and me.

I want to summon up excuses not to do this, but resist the temptation. I am not going to die riding down a country lane, I tell my better self. My worse self is convinced that riding alone increases the chances of this happening exponentially. I explain to my worse self that if Duke bolts because a spaceship lands in Hensting Lane, then being with a friend or instructor isn't going to help. I am the only one who can ride Duke. This is what's worrying me, says my worse self unhelpfully.

I needn't have worried. There are no spaceships landing in Hensting Lane today, or road-filling tractors, or explosions in the hedgerows. Also, Duke is as steady as they come. He spends his days walking up and down this road taking care of disabled riders, so he doesn't bat an eyelid at bicycles or cars, things that I've studied in my road safety exam and now am experiencing first-hand.

I'm just about convinced that he is never scared of anything when suddenly he stands stock still in the road, rigid, and won't move.

He is scared of his own shadow.

A low winter sun has come out from behind the clouds and has thrown dark shadows onto the road. The shadow that daunts him most is his own, which lies, as you might expect, right in his path.

I give him a gentle pat, explaining that this is nothing to be scared of and that, no, he can't veer round it as it will follow him. Which it does when he tries to get away from it. This results in us ending up in the middle of the road in a neat repetition of the exam situation. As there's no traffic coming this isn't a particular concern, but on a double blind bend with a horse who is worried about his own shadow is not the best place to be. So I dredge through what passes for my memory about what to do under such circumstances. Nothing springs to mind, but I do recall how to get the horse to work through a bend for a dressage test. You use your inside leg (in this case, my right one) to give the horse something to bend round. Then you use your outside leg (my left), combined with a slight tweak on the right rein and looking where you're going, to urge him round that leg. I summon this up and, unbelievably, Duke does it, bending his massive flank and side round my right leg, stepping over and past his scary shadow and onto the road ahead. It's a small success.

We stroll past bare winter fields, other horses grazing, a stunning seventeenth-century, Grade-II-listed thatched barn and pretty cottages, and then turn for home. In the hedgerows, winter is still in the ascendant. The frothy seed heads of old man's beard hang from many shrubs and trees, and there are the remains of black bryony with its beautiful, but poisonous, red berries. It's only been half an hour, and I have talked out loud to Duke the whole way like a mad woman, in a bid to stay calm, but it's progress.

Back at the yard, I'm still finding that ordinary chores such as tacking up and mucking out a stable leave me breathless. Lessons too result in me gasping for air. Flick calls out, "Remember to breathe, Hazel" as Duke and I trot round the school and I turn blue. Every ten minutes we stop so that I can gasp for breath, gulping in huge lungfuls of air. Is this normal? If not, then presumably this is what it looks like to be middle-aged and unfit.

Most certainly not, says the asthma nurse. Phil has deployed his medical training to tell me that I have got "a barn-door case of exercise-induced asthma" and has encouraged me to seek a local medical opinion. So I find myself trying to breathe into a tube at the nurse's surgery. The tests don't reveal asthma, and my lung function is good, apparently. Extraordinarily, the nurse also says that I'm very fit. I'd quite like her to write this down so that I can frame it. But the rest of the symptoms of exercise-induced asthma are there. If I do any exercise I'm left puffing and blowing.

I've always been like this. Even in my fabulously fit days as an aerobics queen I would yawn through a class, much to everyone's mirth and amid jokes about keeping me up. When running up the steep hill to my home, at the end of the 5 km run I did three times a week, I would end up unable to breathe and have to stop halfway and walk. Phil and the asthma nurse concur that this was just my body trying to get air into my lungs. I was neither bored nor unfit.

I'm sent home with an inhaler to use twice a day and an emergency one to use when I cough and gasp for breath. I feel extremely chipper that I have a solid-gold excuse for not being able to run up the steep hill on which I live. My lungs won't let me. It's not that I'm a slothful middle-aged woman. I'm not unfit. I'm asthmatic. Hoorah.

The asthma nurse says, "Give it a week, and you won't be breathless." She's right. Formerly, just putting Duke's saddle on led to gasping and a couple of minutes of leaning up against him getting my breath back. Now, I just put it on and walk off to fetch his bridle. It's extraordinary.

This is the only positive bit of medical news for the month, as it turns out. My father's condition continues to deteriorate. In practice this means that he can't remember how to do tasks that he always used to do without thinking.

He's a keen gardener and botanist, but now even their small garden overwhelms him. He can't remember what to do in it or why. His DIY skills have abandoned him. So he sits in his study staring at old botanical paperwork, finding it perplexing, unable to name the plants that he's spent more than thirty years studying. It is heartbreaking. Worse, he hangs around my mother in the kitchen, seeking reassurance. What should he do? How should he do it? She gives him things to do, but then he can't do them. He gets frustrated. She is exhausted.

The local council has come up trumps, however, finding my father a room in a respite care home a few miles away for a week. There are rows as my father insists he won't go. Why should he? And why isn't Mummy coming too?

In the event, it isn't too bad. My mother has a week without the constant demands of someone who still looks like the person she married, but isn't. By the end of the week, a few glasses of red wine, some rest, and catching up on *University Challenge* have brightened her spirits.

Daddy returns home. A few days later I'm driving to work when he starts to call me repeatedly on my mobile phone. I ignore it. For a few years now, as the dementia has worsened, he's been phoning me many times a day. He can't remember his previous calls. He simply lives in a momentary bubble of perplexity.

Once, I picked up the phone (whilst driving) and was stopped by a policeman, who fined me, put points on my driving licence, and explained clearly to me the error of my ways. I have not answered the phone whilst driving since.

It takes an hour and a quarter to get to work. When I'm safely parked and unlikely to be a threat to anyone on the road, I call home. Daddy is beside himself with anxiety. "There's something wrong with Mummy," he says.

Time stops. "Let me speak to her," I say, trying to stay calm.

"I'm not sure what it is, dear," she says indistinctly. "But I can't walk upstairs very well. I had to use my hands. And that was a problem as I was trying to carry two cups of early-morning tea. I had to carry one up and go back for the other. It took a long time. When I got back upstairs the tea was cold. Daddy wasn't very happy about that."

It turns out that she's had a stroke. I sit in the car park with everything going into slow motion. "Don't worry," I say, worrying. "I will call an ambulance. You just stay there. I'll explain to my colleagues that I can't stay at work and then I'll come home. Tell Daddy to wait there and I'll look after him. Then I'll come on to the hospital."

I call 999, trying not to panic. An ambulance is dispatched. I race into the office and tell my lovely boss and an equally lovely girl from HR that I can't stay, as it looks as though my mum's had a stroke.

Then I turn round and pretty much break the land speed record down the M4. I get to my parents' home more quickly than I would have thought possible. The door is locked. No one is there. I am frantic with worry. Where is my father? He's been banned from driving because of his dementia, but refuses to take this on board and so we have to hide the car keys to stop him.

Nonetheless, neither he nor the car is anywhere to be seen. The neighbours saw the ambulance. They know my mother's gone. But my father? No one knows.

Then a small yellow car draws up. It's my dad. I shout at him.

"Where have you been? Why were you driving? I have been out of my mind with worry." The irony that I sound like the parent is not lost on me, but I'm not laughing. Neither is he. He is childlike in his answer.

"Well, there wasn't any bacon for breakfast, so I went to get some."

I am undone. His wife of nearly fifty years has just been taken to hospital with a stroke, but, because of his dementia, all my dad can work out is that there isn't any bacon (actually there is, if you look) and so he breaks the law of the road too and drives off to buy some. Dear God, how many parents am I going to lose today?

I cook the bacon with bad grace and, once he's eating, head off to the local hospital, hiding the yellow car's keys to prevent a repeat incident. There is a blur of doctors, nurses, questions, people, and then a quiet side room with my mother looking more ill and old than I can bear.

In a moment, everything has changed. The future looks perilous.

Born in 1928 in rural Buckinghamshire, my mother went to Cambridge to study to be a teacher at the end of the war, aged just seventeen. From these happy years she learned enough to provide insightful, interesting, fun teaching for nursery and primary school children for the rest of her career. I was in her class aged just four, and can testify to how enjoyable it was. From her own quiet, loving mother, she learned compassion, gentleness, and care, and she has an inbuilt interest in others that makes her endlessly giving, kind, and fascinated by other people's lives.

Everyone loves her, not just Daddy and me. She may be small (4'11 and ¾ and shrinking) but she has bright, twinkly blue eyes, a ready smile, rosy cheeks, and an encouraging word for everyone. My friends refer to her as "Mrs Tiggiwinkle". She calls them "dear". She lights up every room she walks into and has no idea at all that people treasure her as much as they do, which makes them love her all the more.

At university, I was always at my most popular when my parents had visited, my mother bearing a home-made fruit cake. It would be devoured in minutes after their departure by the ravening hordes of friends who had seen them arrive.

But today there is no light left within her. She looks grey, worried, and defeated. I hold her hand and try to be encouraging and bright, as she has taught me. "Don't worry," I say. "The prognosis is good. You're going to recover from this. Your job is just to rest. I'll look after everything else."

For forty-eight hours I move into my parents' home and take on my mother's life. I sleep in her bed. Their cat Polly, distressed by her mistress's absence, tries to sleep on top of me at night. She gets short shrift.

So does my father. Dementia has slowed him down so much that he is perpetually tired. He sleeps for much of the day in a chair in the sitting room. So at night, though he is tired and retires early, he cannot sleep. This results in him taking unspecified quantities of sleeping tablets that I didn't know he had. So by morning it is impossible to wake him. If I've got him up and dressed by noon, I consider it a triumph.

But because he then sorely needs the normal structure of a day, the whole day is moved back (for him) by five or six hours. He has breakfast at lunchtime, then wants lunch mid-afternoon, closely followed by dinner and bed. In between times he doesn't know what's happening; where Mummy is; what's going on; or how to do any of the things that he normally would. He is utterly bewildered. If I explain it all, five minutes later I'll be explaining it again. And I am. I know it's not his fault, but it is frustrating and nerve-jangling. I snap at him. He snaps back. Most of the time I want to scream.

After forty-eight hours I know two things for sure: I can't carry on like this and neither can my mother. How she has coped for six years is baffling. We have reached the moment at which we need professional help. Government cuts have meant that, already, some 500,000 people like my parents no longer have access to care, according to the Alzheimer's Society. Cuts that come as I'm writing this book mean that a further 330,000 people are affected. Presumably, like my mother, many of them are also at their wits' end.

I ring the nice lady at social services and explain. She understands and visits my mother in hospital. Her considered opinion is that, if my mother is to have a chance of recovery, she needs time apart from my father. So it is arranged that he will go into temporary care, back at the friendly respite centre, for a few weeks in order to give her a chance to get over the stroke. The manager at the respite centre advises me that the best way to do this is simply to bring him with a suitcase of his things and explain it on the way. He's going to find it hard enough to understand, she says, without you having to endlessly repeat what's happening.

It sounds wise. But as I wake up on the third day I feel that I'm tricking him into going into care. Also, in my heart of hearts, I know that he won't come home from this. Temporary care will be a stepping stone to permanent care. This will be his last day at home, the last day of his life as he has always known it. He doesn't know it, but I do.

By late morning he is up and breakfasted, despite a night of poor sleep and tablets. He heads for his beloved greenhouse and potters about watering his plants, slowly, methodically – his body somehow remembering old habits.

"I won't be very long," he says, heading out. "I just need to water everything."

"You take your time," I say, feeling duplicitous. I sit indoors watching him, and weep. Inexplicably we have come to a fork in the road where I now feel that I have a very real choice between saving one parent or the other, but not both.

Later I'll come to understand that putting my father into care is the only kind thing to do for him. It will keep him safe. He won't wander off into the village and get lost, as he has been doing. He won't drive off in the car any longer and cause who-knows-what kind of dreadful accident. We won't find him in a ditch in the early hours of the morning if he walks off at night. He won't fall down the stairs, set the kitchen alight by leaving a pan on the stove, or take so many sleeping pills that he ends up in hospital.

This, I'll realize, is the path that everyone in our position treads. It is not malevolent – as it feels right now – but a kind thing to do this. It doesn't represent a lack of love, but a new kind of care. But right now I feel that we are running from a war zone where the battle is encroaching upon our lives. We are fleeing our home. My father is wounded. And I am leaving him at the fork in the road and continuing ahead with my mother, letting him die alone by the roadside. Never let it be said, therefore, that it is an easy choice to put your parent into care. There are 433,000 people currently living in care homes in the UK. Every one of them is loved by someone, and that someone has had a very difficult decision to take indeed.

I put Daddy's suitcase in the back of the car and we drive, silently, to the respite care home. He thinks he's coming home. I know it's likely that he isn't. Everyone is very kind and welcoming. He brightens at this, likes his room, and we sit outside in the sunshine drinking orange juice.

The centre's manager nods at me to leave while my father isn't looking, just as the parent of a small child leaves them at school quietly and unobserved.

It works, temporarily. Then the phone calls start. Because he can't remember why he's there, Daddy rings me to find out. When the call is over, he forgets that he's rung and what I've said.

So he rings again.

On bad days, he rings every fifteen minutes. He gets angrier and angrier as his perplexity grows. I explain and explain that Mummy has had a stroke; that she needs time to recover alone.

"I could help," he says. But he couldn't. And that's a tough one to counter, because he is certain that he could.

"Why am I in prison?" he shouts at me. "I will commit suicide if you don't come and bring me home right away."

No pressure, then.

I get in the car. My destination, however, is not the care home of an allegedly suicidal father, but the hospital and my mother. It's time to bring her home and I have to believe that, despite his threats, my father will not kill himself.

It takes a long time to get the necessary permissions for my mother to leave hospital, as she is feeling sick, dizzy, and weak. But finally I do get her home. On the basis that there is nowhere as restful as your own bed, this has to be a good thing.

But she is weak and wobbly, physically and emotionally. The physical effects of the stroke are clear: most obviously, she can't write. As a schoolteacher, she had beautiful, copperplate handwriting, perfect for writing on blackboards, and utterly familiar to me from a lifetime of letters and hastily-written notes. I pretend everything is fine and bottle up my shock.

By the end of the month, she dispatches me back to my house to "do something that you want to, dear". I'm sufficiently confident that she'll cope for forty-eight hours that I agree to do this. First, kindly friends come round to help with my garden, which has been ignored all month and is thus somewhat jungle-like in appearance.

Then everyone stays for dinner, and my friend Keith joins us from London and another friend, Jim, from the USA. The plan is that Keith, Phil, and Clare will run a local half-marathon the next day. We're enjoying a jolly evening when the phone rings. It's my father. He has rung earlier in the day and four times the day before, but can't remember any of it. He accuses me, fiercely, of not telling him what is going on.

Something within me snaps. Patience. Nerve. Endurance. The ability to recite repeatedly and calmly what's happening and why. I become completely hysterical and sit in the bathroom babbling incoherently down the phone to my father, who is incoherent back.

A dreadful hush falls on the assembled company. Clare comes running from the dining room. "He doesn't understand, Hazel," she says, wisely.

This is what you forget when you have a parent with dementia. He still looks like my dad, sounds like my dad – though that will fade – but he isn't my dad any longer. He can't react as he used to, or understand as he formerly did. That's hard for me to remember.

At this point, in my life as a newspaper journalist, there would be a photograph of our family years ago, with the caption "In happier times".

There were plenty of happier times before dementia took my father away. He was born in 1933 in a house overlooking the common in the village where we all grew up. As village football matches were played here, he swears it gave him a life-long passion for the beautiful game.

Despite attending a local grammar school where rugby was played, he never took to it and instead ended up captaining the village football team. Brutal matches against neighbouring village sides were watched over by elderly residents who couldn't understand it when the home side lost. You could tell who you were playing, my dad used to say, by their accent. Just sixty years ago, a squad from a village three or four miles away would have a markedly different accent.

On more than one occasion, referees who made decisions against the home team were given an early bath in the village pond. This resulted in a ban from the league that was quietly forgotten during World War Two. The village team wasn't, however, the rural equivalent of Millwall. But they were tough players, taking their post-match baths in a farmer's sheep-dip run.

My father's own father was a milkman who did his rounds with a horse and cart. His mother was in service in the kitchens of a big house. (Think "downstairs" in *Downton Abbey* and you've about got it.) But my father was bright and excelled at Greek and Latin at school. His teacher wanted him to do Classics at Oxbridge. Financially, this simply wasn't an option, so my dad left school at eighteen and got a job with what was then the General Electric Company.

His happiest years were spent as a radar fitter for the RAF, based all round the UK, but most memorably on the Isle of Lewis in the Outer Hebrides.

Here, as well as working, he'd watch migrating birds on the radar whilst on night shift, play the local lads at football, and spend hours studying the local fauna and flora. Once he even had a go at horse riding. But the pony concerned bolted with him, and that was the end of my father's equine adventures.

His rural upbringing meant that he was completely conversant with what grew and lived around him. He was endlessly curious about new plants and birds. My memories of early childhood are dotted with strange avian episodes, such as being taken to listen to a nightjar singing in the dark (it didn't show up), ringing migrating birds in the back garden in mist nets, and my father sitting on my grandfather's roof during the Wimbledon men's final with a shotgun, to stop the starlings getting the annual cherry crop.

Cherries and the wood from the trees were the big local crops in our village. During my father's childhood, everything stopped for the cherry harvest. Children didn't attend school; adults sloped off work until every cherry was in and sold. A man, my father used to say, would show his virility and fitness by the length of cherry ladder that he could carry through the orchards.

This was done hand above hand with the ladder upright in front of you. Really strong blokes, my dad said, could carry a seventy-two-rung ladder. He was less forthcoming about what he could carry. Even as a small child, I could carry a twenty-four-rung ladder.

Later, his curiosity about wildlife led him to study a family of plants that include cow parsley, known as *Umbelliferae*. Driving down our road in the village one day, he wondered why one white-flowered plant was different from another. No one could tell him, so he set out to discover the differences himself.

It was a journey that was to take him initially round Britain and then across Europe and into Turkey. Every summer holiday revolved around climbing mountains looking for plants. Seeds were brought home and grown in the greenhouse. Plants were pressed in old, faded, foreign newspapers.

In the end, this quiet, solitary man from Buckinghamshire became one of the leading experts on these plants from across Europe and beyond. He had an encyclopedic memory for the hundreds of different varieties and people would send him plants (or fragments of them) from around the world to identify.

"How am I meant to identify this plant from a handful of broken pieces?" he'd moan. But a few days later he'd have the answer, every time.

His wartime childhood left a mark, however, and not just in the *Rupert Bear* annuals in which he'd drawn aeroplane dog fights. The war gave my father a make-do-and-mend attitude. He could fix anything with anything. It assuredly wouldn't look beautiful, and it probably wouldn't be straight, but it would work.

Once, during a particularly hot summer, keen to conserve what water there was, he not only installed eleven water butts but also dug a well in the garden… with a trowel. This must have been a considerable shock for a representative of the MORI poll who called to ask what my parents were doing to save water. I bet he didn't have a box on his tick-sheet for "dug a well".

When he wasn't working (and certainly after he retired) my father's life was spent in the garden and the greenhouse. He'd read *The Guardian* from cover to cover six days a week, eschewing *The Observer* on Sundays in favour of going to church. He was a man of very profound faith. Though ill health had dogged him for much of his adult life, he had retained an unshakeable love of God, and a belief that God loved him in return. The Bible was the only book beside his bed and he would quote from it regularly. Though he grew up attending church, it wasn't until his Air Force years that he became a Christian, taking up the faith personally and with commitment. He tried to implement what he read in the Bible in his dealings with others, was a regular attendee at the tiny local chapel, and, put simply, trusted God.

He kept a small, torn, yellowing piece of paper in his desk. It was from an old calendar that gave a Bible verse for each day. The day in question was 16 August 1963, just a few weeks after my parents had married and more than a year before my birth. The verse came from Isaiah 46:4 and reads, "I will be your God through all your lifetime." He clung to that, and it remained true despite what he was going through now.

My father also loved everything written by Bach, thought novels and television a waste of time, held firmly left-wing political views, and enjoyed a rollicking good laugh with his next-door neighbour and fellow gardener, Peter.

Now all this was gone. We hadn't quite got to the stage where he couldn't remember my name, though this was to come. When I looked at my father, I knew all these things and remembered them. When he looked in the mirror, he could not recall them. His past was a foreign land; his present a confusing one.

April

"A pinch and a punch, the first day of the month," we used to say at school, pinching and punching cruelly. Today's pinch and punch came in the form of a meeting with social services about Daddy's care.

Because my mother comes from a generation that was brought up never to complain, she doesn't, even now, despite everything. So I have to school her in explaining to social services that she is not coping, has had a complete physical collapse, is emotionally strung out, and, quite simply, can't look after my dad any more.

She is resistant to the idea of saying any of this. I beg her. "Please," I say, "if it's just me stating that he needs to go into care, they'll think I'm a callous daughter who doesn't care about her parents. If *you* say that you can't cope, they'll see the need." She remains unconvinced.

I am not sleeping, owing to worry about the pending meeting. It haunts me day and night. What if the social workers say that Daddy can go home? After all, the recession has meant a cut in budgets. They can't look after everyone. However, I know we cannot cope if Daddy comes home. I am convinced that it will lead to my mother's death.

Phil, ever rational, talks me through how the meeting will go, what I will say. The social workers do care, he says. And of course, as always, he is right. The lead social worker (how did we get to a place where we have several social workers?) is convinced that if my father returned home it would jeopardize my mother's health, leading to a second stroke and possibly her death.

She understands that my father is unaware of this. But, for her, that is not an issue. What needs to happen now, the lead social worker says, is that my father stays on at the respite care home and that we then try to find a long-term home for him.

Sadly, this can't be the respite care home, because his room isn't en suite. I say that he slummed it in who-knows-what conditions in the RAF and won't be at all bothered. This won't do, the social workers say. They don't tell me, but what they are trying not to say is that soon my dad will need his own toilet nearby because he will become incontinent. His ailing memory will forget to send the not-just-yet signals to his bladder and bowels, with repeatedly messy consequences. He will return to wearing nappies. Later, I'm glad that they didn't tell me. It is an awful thing to watch your father lose his dignity. Right now, I'm just frustrated by this piece of news.

But, despite this, the deal is done surprisingly easily. I had thought I would have to fight, beg, and plead for care for my father (and circuitously for my mother). But I don't. It is, it would seem, a foregone conclusion. Even my mother manages to explain that she doesn't have a grip on her emotions; that she is completely wrecked by my father's constant calls begging to come home; that she isn't sleeping; that she is in pieces.

We try to head Daddy's phone calls off at the pass. It is agreed that I will phone him every evening, allowing him the chance to vent his frustrations and anger at me. All inbound calls will go to my mother's answerphone. She will delete the ones from him and ring him for a chat at the weekend.

It's the kind of plan that you put in place when you don't realize how bad dementia gets. Of course, it doesn't work, but it's worth a try. My mother reports that she can't sleep and, if she does finally drop off, she wakes later with what she describes as "indigestion", a pain in her chest that keeps her awake. All manner of alarm bells are ringing in my head. Does this mean that she is about to have another stroke? What happens then? Phil says that indigestion can be brought on by fraught emotional circumstances. I remind myself that he is never wrong, and grit my teeth. Today my mother will not die. Today my father is safe.

But at home alone, with no one there to be upset by my doing so, I weep uncontrollably. I cannot stop crying. I cry so much that my contact lenses come out. I am awash with sorrow.

If this were fiction – and would that it were – about now there would be a storm. Rain would pour down for days in a deluge. The sky would be black and lowering. Rivers would break their banks. It might even be unusually cold. Back in my schooldays, this was absolutely my favourite literary device: the pathetic fallacy – weather that reflected what was going on in the lives or emotions of the characters. Thanks to an excellent English teacher, Miss Woodhouse, when I was thirteen I thought that that was about the coolest thing there was. (I didn't get out much.)

Actually, more than thirty years on, I still think it's fabulous. Who, after all, isn't cheered by the sight of a rainbow? And don't we all chat to passers-by more when the sun is out?

But this is not fiction. So we are not experiencing biblical downpours. Instead, the sun is shining. It is unnaturally warm, in the manner of an increasing number of spring days. On the one hand, I love it. On the other, reporting about global warming tells me that this is Not A Good Thing. But good weather means that it is possible to get out and away from it all on Duke. I head for the yard on a glorious spring day. It's warm, sunny, and blue-skied. Every kind of blossom is out in the hedgerows: pear, cherry, blackthorn, and even the pink-hued apple, my personal favourite. The hedgerows are billowing with whiteness and the promise of a delicious harvest, if we avoid late frosts.

In what remains of my memory I am trying to store the places where different trees grow so that I may return in August, September, and October to harvest the fruit. There are tiny lanes hereabouts where old orchards grow untended and forgotten. My father and I have spent many a happy hour gathering plums, damsons, and bullace (one down from a plum; one up from a sloe), as well as the yellow-and-red-coloured wild cherry plums. I have made pots and pots of jam and chutney from them over the years. In the autumn, we would harvest pounds of sloes to make sloe gin. And the late spring would see us heading out to pick elderflower heads for cordial.

My father has been marking an old Ordnance Survey map with what grows where. He won't do it any more. We won't be foraging together again. Now it is up to me to remember and log where everything grows, my job to harvest the resultant crops. The fun has gone out of it, but I will do it for him, if for nothing else. So, as I drive to the stables, I mentally clock what is where: blackberries on both sides, particularly on the first bend, though so high up I may need to pick them from Duke's back; sloes further up to the right and in the woods; cobnuts on the corner by the cornfield. "I will return," I say to the trees. "Your blossom tells me where you are. I will see you all in late summer."

Duke and I head off down the road, surrounded by the billowing whiteness. Looking at the blossom makes me feel hopeful for the first time in a while. This improves my riding. I am not slumped in the saddle in despair; I'm looking up and out at the absolute glory of the world. This transmits itself to Duke, who is bright and upbeat too. International riders will tell you that you have to sell every manoeuvre to a horse. We may not be jumping five-foot competition fences, but if I can sell Duke a pleasant-but-determined walk in the countryside, so much the better for our partnership. As this is Duke's patch, and frankly, he could do it with his eyes closed, I attempt to improve his walk and trot from just ticking along to what is known as having a contact.

This essentially means that the horse is listening to you. You aren't cruising along like a person on a four-legged living sofa; the horse is concentrating and doing your bidding. But it's a bit more than that. By putting pressure through your legs into his sides, you force the horse forward. But then you control that energy through your hands, encouraging the horse to lower his head. When he does this he really has to work, striding out, pushing himself along with his hind legs, not slopping along, dragging himself from the front. It is, if you like, the difference between strolling and power-walking for a human. It's called being in an outline, or contact work. It makes Duke fitter, gets him concentrating, and is more of a workout than a saunter.

Our attempts at contact work in the school have not been covered in glory, purely because I really haven't cared whether Duke does it or not. I haven't sold it to either myself or him. He's known that and has taken the easy option of not doing it. Why work hard if you don't have to? And why would I care? Simply going forward and then being able to stop at the appropriate time has been enough. Let's not get technical about it. Plus, I have had one or two other more important things on my mind.

But today, with the sun shining, everything seems possible. So I push through my legs, squeeze gently with my hands, and down goes his mighty head. He powers through each stride, fairly chewing up the road. It's a completely different feeling. This is the difference between actually riding a horse and sitting on one while it moves. Let's not be too triumphant, though: it only happens for half the fifteen-minute journey home when Duke knows that there are both carrots and Polo mints waiting for him back at the yard. But, nonetheless, it happens.

Encouraged, I decide to ride the next day with my friends Annie and Kirsten. Annie has on loan Duke's equivalent, Lady, the Shire horse; and Kirsten has Blue Eyes, a small black-and-white cob with issues. They are both tremendous horses. Lady will go on to compete in both showing and dressage at county level. Blue Eyes will deploy all his intelligence in competing at a national level. Right now, we don't know any of this. We're just glad of the chance of a hack in the countryside. Annie and Kirsten are work pals. Both of them rode when they were children, and just recently vowed to get back into the saddle after years away. They've been having lessons, like me, but have soon progressed to having horses on loan, their original aim.

They are a tonic: full of laughter, funny stories, words of encouragement, and, quite frequently, a verbal kick up the backside. They refuse to let me believe that I can't ride. Annie is positive, smiling, with shoulder-length curly, dark hair. She is beautiful inside and out. Everyone who meets her likes her. Kirsten has a can-do attitude towards everything. She believes utterly in her ability to beguile Blue Eyes, ride well, and do anything else successfully. She brooks no nonsense from me and so is a joy to be with. She is the most stylish of the three of us, riding in matching outfits and snappy dark sunglasses.

It is more like May than April when we leave the yard, with the temperature topping out at 22 degrees. We head out through the woods, where the winter's rain followed by the current warmth has meant that spring has definitely sprung. A hint of green is everywhere on the trees and more sloes are giving themselves away as frothy splashes of white in the solemnity of the beech woods.

We decide to track snake-like up and across the woods and then out through a barley field towards a pub before turning for home. This takes us to the edge of Marwell Zoo's woodland, an area that has been continuously wooded for at least 300 years, but probably far, far more. Its woodland team has recently started the process of thinning out the upper storey of trees to let more light in and that light is resulting in carpets of flowers at the woodland's edge. All is going well, with Lady and Blue Eyes leading the way and Duke just following, until he spots Something That Wasn't There Before. This is always nerve-racking for a horse. It can be anything: a flapping plastic bag caught in the hedgerow, the stump of a newly-felled tree, or, in this case, a clump of primroses that has flowered since the last time we came along this route. The primroses are newly open, spurred into bloom by the light let in by the pruning of the trees.

Duke's eyes are out, appropriately enough, on stalks. Every muscle within him tenses against this potential danger. What is this fearsome thing by the side of the path, he's thinking? And how can I pass it without injury? He stands stock still in case the primroses should pounce on him; snorts at them; stares them down; and will not move. I nudge him with my legs. Nothing. I nudge a bit more. Still nothing. Then I give a proper Pony Club kick in the manner of a child in a Thelwell cartoon and we pass the fearsome primroses, our lives somehow still preserved.

It is *infra dig* to admit that your horse is scared of primroses and that you in turn are scared by your horse's reaction to primroses, so I say nothing. But Duke and I are a little quivery when we come to the huge barley field that leads to the pub. There is a wide, flat track up the middle of the field, beloved of horse riders locally as it gives them the chance to let their horses have a good canter or gallop. As Duke is on restricted jollity to preserve his hooves and prevent pain, we are limited to a trot. So Annie and Kirsten send us on ahead, intending to leave a gap and then come roaring up behind us like the Mongol hordes.

Duke does not take well to the idea of going first when he

has been having an easy time of it at the rear of the ride. At the back all he has to do is follow the horse in front. Ahead, he has to be alert to any dangers that may threaten the three horses. But, with some effort, I encourage him past his pals and explain to him, through use of my inner calf, that we are going to trot up this field and we are going to do so first. At this point we have a difference of opinion. Out of the corner of his right eye, Duke spots ostriches. Hampshire isn't exactly awash with ostrich farms, but we are alongside Marwell Zoo, and so have a free safari. There are waterbuck (a type of antelope), giraffe, and Grévy's zebra too. But it's the ostriches that are the real problem. Duke doesn't like it when a pigeon emerges unexpectedly from a hedgerow. Just imagine his shock now when a flock of ostriches do so. The horror.

There is only one thing to do, in his mind, and that is run for it. It doesn't matter that there is a fence between us and the ostriches, and half the enormous barley field too. So he heads off at a canter, sideways through the young barley crop. I don't know how to canter sideways. I have no idea how we are doing this. Normally it's hard enough to get me over my fear of speed and into the gait in the first place, but sideways? I've seen it done in the dressage arena but always intentionally, with skill, grace, and control.

This has none of those. We're just flattening crops at speed in a bid to get away from the ostriches. My options are to let this continue and then somehow end up back in the woods, but without Annie and Kirsten, or to get a hold of three-quarters of a tonne of nervous horse and come back onto the track. I opt for the latter, throwing all of my eight-stone weight down the left-hand side of my body to try to prevent him going that way. I look towards the path, turn my shoulders to it, and will him to go back there. And suddenly we are back, trotting, going straight up the path, the ostriches behind us, with Annie and Kirsten, roaring with laughter, pounding up behind us.

It wasn't our finest hour. But as we stroll back down the long, winding path through the woods, my heart sings with the simple joy of being outside and away from everything. The woods are carpeted with bluebells, and though it is only early April, they are beginning to come out, encouraged by the unseasonal warmth. There are vast swathes of celandines, dandelions, and white wood anemones, glittering star-like beneath the trees. Soon there will be Solomon's seal and wood spurge along the lighter edges of the tracks.

Back at the yard we have progress of a different sort. Duke now lifts his feet one at a time to have them picked out after a ride. This was initially a trial of strength and will, as he planted his feet and simply refused to raise them. But as I've got gentler, he's acquiesced to having his hooves picked out, and now, post-ride, I can check for stones and mud (of which we have plenty) and leave him clean-shod before going home. It is an indication of trust.

Buoyed and uplifted, I drive to my mother's house to take her out for lunch. I'm not convinced that she's eating much, because she's too tired to cook, so I want to get a decent meal inside her. I find her in the garden, where she has fallen through a deck chair and has taken ten minutes to get up on her feet again. She tries to laugh it off but is badly shaken. Away fly the relief, buoyancy, and joy. Back come the anxiety, fear, and worry.

We go out to lunch anyway. She's shaken, but getting out gives perspective as well as food, and by the end of the hour we're both finding things to laugh at, though not her tumble. The respite care home reports that my father has been "phone-happy" and, sure enough, on our return my mother's answerphone is chock-full of messages from him: threatening, furious, frustrated, lost. We delete them. But neither of us sleeps much that night.

I'm averaging about two hours' sleep per night, which doesn't leave me at my best in the mornings. My nerves are frayed before I visit my dad. They get more frayed when I'm there. He is of the opinion that Mummy and I have what he calls "a fixed view" of the situation and that we "just want to dump" him. We go round this several times. I really want him to understand that this isn't the case; that we are broken and can't go on; that we love him, but we can't cope with his increasing needs; that he is safer where he is; that we will visit almost every day.

He is intransigent. We are the enemy, not family now. We have not behaved lovingly. He will threaten us back into dutiful submission. Order, the old order, will be restored. I can't bear it. My father's will has always been the driving force in our family. What he said happened. We didn't argue; it wasn't worth it. My father would brook no argument, no opposition. We have been submissive.

Not any more. I understand that he has no concept of what is happening. But I am hurt by weeks of antagonistic phone calls. There will be no more manipulation. "I'm sorry if you really believe that to be the case," I say. "I can't change your mind, no matter what I say, so I'm going home, because I don't want to be talked to like this any more."

It's taken more than forty years to stand up to him. Mummy is doing the same. When my father calls and threatens suicide again if he is not brought home immediately, she tells him – twice – that he is being selfish, failing to consider how such statements make her feel. Then she puts the phone down. We can't believe we're doing it. We hate doing it. But we feel backed into a corner – not by my dad, whom we love, but by the illness, which is changing all of our lives, and us with it.

In the midst of all of this, work somehow happens. Clare and I head for Scotland on an assignment that goes well. We discover a story in the Côte d'Ivoire that needs telling, and get a commission from *Geographical* magazine and an expression of real interest from *The Sunday Times*. It's not enough for the aid agency whose story it is, and, as quickly as it was on, the trip is off.

It always leaves me feeling deflated when this happens, as it sometimes does. But you can't make a foreign assignment work if it's simply not going to. You have to be philosophical and recognize that other stories will come. You will return to Heathrow Airport. But this time I feel more down about it than usual. I haven't had a holiday in six years as my father's health has deteriorated, but I will allow myself to jump on a plane for work purposes. A break right now – if only to report other people's suffering – would have been welcome. But it would also have been selfish.

Duke looks at me over the half-door of his stable and seems glad that I've not gone anywhere. If I turn up three or four times a week and groom him, he gets time out of lessons and rides for the rest of the yard's customers. So I represent a bit of a breather, as well as being the purveyor of carrots. Also, it is with me that he gets off-road and into the woods, which I'm convinced he loves just as much as I do. I want to be kind to him and I am trying. But sometimes I know that I am so consumed with my own emotions that I don't have much left for him.

However, as the sun is still shining – this being fact, not fiction – we take ourselves out to the woods again. It is a ten-minute ride along the lane and then up a sharp, steep chalk track before you get into the heart of the woods. I hate that track. It is narrow, sometimes little wider than the horse. On one side it drops away into a deep, dug-out chalk pit. If we slipped and fell down there, it would be goodnight all, as my grandmother used to say.

At its lowest point, the chalk pit is sixty feet deep and covers

0.4 hectares, which is 43,000 square feet. A local farmer owns it now, but no one really knows its history, except to say that it is the largest of the chalk pits that dot the area. We are at a place where the predominant heavy clay meets a ridge of chalk, hence the chalk pits. For centuries, possibly for thousands of years, back to Roman times, this chalk pit would have been dug out by hand. The chalk would then be scattered to improve the productivity of the fields, which are, the farmer tells me, a bit too acidic. He buys in chalk-based products to do the same thing these days. But for many a long year men did this by hand in order to grow wheat, barley, and oats in the surrounding fields. These were tough men and it's a very, very big hole. There are trees growing at the bottom that are now fifty to sixty years old. Badger setts ring the top of the pit, which is a happy hunting ground for tawny, barn, and little owls.

But I'm not good with heights, so when I look down I am shaken by the sheer drop that falls away to my left. The farmer tells me that people have fallen down it and survived. I don't want to put that to the test, particularly on Duke. Riding up feels less risky than going downhill, though there is a deep rut forming in the centre of the track, giving little room to ride either to left or right. But forward momentum keeps us going up, rather than down, I reckon. Nonetheless, I am nervous about bringing Duke down there. As his front feet are weak and have a tendency to lameness, he finds it hard to put pressure on them. He's got special, wedged shoes on his front hooves, to cushion some of the blow, but even so, I can feel his hesitancy about walking down any slope, let alone a steep one like this.

So we go up it, not down. And, my goodness, it's worth it in late April. The woods are carpeted in English bluebells that stretch away into the distance. The bluebells are at their best: fully out, highly scented. We walk to a point along the path where all we can see is bluebells in any direction, and stop. Perhaps because his feet hurt, Duke finds standing still very difficult. We've been practising standing still to the count of three seconds, then four, then five, and so on. Part of it, I'm sure, is that we both need to be relaxed enough to stand still. My soul needs to stop fizzing with stress. And I need to stop passing on that stress and fear to him, because it makes him want to bolt for home.

If you ever feel you can't stand still, surround yourself with bluebells and you will find peace and the ability just to stand and stare. Accordingly, Duke and I stand there – or, to be more accurate, Duke stands and I sit on his back – and gaze and gaze at the vast expanse of bluebells. We do this for several minutes, not seconds. I try to drink the view in as if I would never see anything like this again. I want to bottle the beauty, and the quietness. No one is around. Very often, I meet dog walkers, other riders, the occasional off-road cyclist, or a particularly keen cross-country runner. Not today. There is no one. Robins hop about in the lower branches of the hazel stands. A few rabbits lollop across our path, descendants presumably of a huge rabbit farm that was here in Henry VIII's time. Finally, I sigh, gather the reins and my thoughts, and we walk slowly on, stiller inside and quieter.

The quietness breeds confidence, as I manage my first gate. I appreciate that opening gates is easy if you're on the ground. But it's not as easy when you are reaching down from the back of a horse, when you are at least five feet up in the air and not very supple. We come to the gate that leads out of the woods. Duke has been going through this gate for ten years and can't believe how slow I am at opening it. I put the reins and whip in one hand and reach down, fumbling for the latch. It goes in and out of my grasp as Duke shuffles about, which is another reason why we need to practise standing still. Finally, I get a purchase on it and he surges forward, his huge chest barrelling through the gate, opening it as an act of will. It's not tidy, but it's effective.

But the next gate floors me. Working out how to open it astride a horse is too much like a Rubik's Cube for me to cope with. It's a simple five-bar gate with a stiff pull handle, and a rope that loops back over the fence post. I look at it, bemused. Which way do I point the horse? Towards the latch, presumably, but straight on to it, or sideways? Once I've got hold of the latch (which I can't do because it's too low for me at this height), how do I get Duke to move away from the gate, while taking the gate with me? And then how do I get him through it, while holding on to it? And how do I close it?

This is where dressage moves would come in handy. Dressage might look like people making horses dance, but the moves originated in battle. If you could train your horse to raise its front legs, march in a pronounced way, or extend its legs, you might avoid dead bodies, or living ones bearing weapons. It's also good for opening gates in the countryside.

I love dressage. I love the precision of it, the teamwork, the control. It's like maths, or music: there is a beauty to it. Duke and I haven't left the starting blocks on dressage yet, but I'm learning a few basic moves: making the horse go right or left with his rear legs while keeping his front legs still; stepping his front legs over each other while moving his rear end round; walking backwards. All of these might be helpful now, if only I could remember how to do them.

I look at the gate and fail to remember anything. Duke looks at the gate and thinks he'll open it without help from me if he has to, and pushes. But it's a big gate and doesn't give, despite his strength. I dismount, open the gate, walk Duke through, and then get back on. At this point, let me tell you, the angels are singing, or laughing, or possibly both. Getting on from the ground is generally, as I've mentioned, extremely difficult for me. Flick had made me do it again and again whilst out hacking, with me cursing her gently under my breath, sweating and generally making a meal of it. But I don't have to get on from the ground. I can use the gate. It takes a couple of attempts as I try to persuade Duke to stand still next to the gate while I scramble up it, which is not part of his usual itinerary. But he works out what I'm attempting to do and stands still, and I clamber aboard. We saunter home down the track to the yard, with me scratching his neck for being such a good chap, and mentally giving myself a pat on the back too.

Here, just for the record, is what you're meant to do in order to open a gate. You approach the gate, but don't let your horse face it, in case they take it as a challenge and jump it! (Yikes. I discover this after four years of having Duke face gates. This is where I've been going wrong.) You ride alongside the gate and halt, with your horse's head just past the catch. In an ideal world you then put your reins and whip in your outside hand, and open the latch with your other hand.

You then push the gate open and walk through slowly, leaning forward and keeping hold of both horse and gate. You turn your horse around, taking care not to bang his backside on the gatepost. You ask your horse to walk forwards so that you can shut the gate, which you do holding the gate in one hand and the horse's reins in the other. At this point you will automatically be awarded a medal. Or, failing that, someone will turn up and say, "Oh, I could have done that for you; I'm going that way," and you will want to scream.

We have one more ride before the end of the month: fifty minutes by ourselves through the woods. If I didn't get a medal for remounting the horse from a gate, I'm of the firm opinion that I should get one for this. Less than four months ago I'd never ridden alone, never been responsible for myself and a horse on a hack, and now we're going out for nearly an hour by ourselves. I don't think that Zara Tindall has anything to worry about just yet, but I'm really pleased with our progress. The fact that we're doing this is a sign that I'm worrying less about riding. But, of course, I am still nervous. This transmits itself to Duke, who is more nervous too when we are out alone in the woods. He looks about him all the time, alert, concerned. Is there something to worry about out there? Are there any more dastardly ostriches or menacing primroses?

There are not. He stares at things just to check that they mean no harm, but I never feel that he is about to bolt for home. Instead, we trot happily up what's commonly referred to as the pink path, through the bluebells, rejoicing in the freedom and the beauty.

To our left, beyond a mixed hedgerow and hazel stands, is a vast field Into Which We Mustn't Go. This is the equine equivalent of Eve and the apple: it's very tempting. We stand and look at it, but don't venture forth. If the police can stop me when I'm answering the phone when driving, logic suggests that the landowner will emerge just as Duke and I are having a crafty trot across the field.

A field may not look particularly interesting, but this one, as with so much of this area, has a story to tell. It's probably been a field continuously for 500, maybe even 1,000, years. Imagine how fabulous the soil must be. Today, half of it is used to grow hay (mixed with sorrel and red clover) for the animals up at the zoo, which is a few hundred yards away. The other half is being turned into a habitat. Little trees are being planted to recreate a shelter belt that clearly existed on the maps of the region from 1872. In time, this will give the barn, small, and tawny owls that live in the woods somewhere fresh to perch. From here, they'll be able to swoop down and pick up lunch in the form of field mice that live in the long, deliberately unkempt edges of the field. Right at the top, in an area that we couldn't reach however rule-breaking we were, there will be wild flowers: great for bees and butterflies. It's beautiful.

It's also the place where Flick traditionally makes me dismount and remount from the ground. We stop. Flick isn't there. I don't have to dismount and remount if I don't want to. And I don't. So we go on without any of this getting-off-and-on-again nonsense. I feel like a child who has refused to do their homework and got away with it. We ride on, with me quietly rejoicing.

Back at the yard, Duke is becoming more affectionate. I've discovered that if I kiss him on the nose, he dozes off. I realize that this doesn't sound like a grand passion, but it's an improvement on lashing his tail in my face and planting his feet and refusing to move. So, back from our final ride of the month, we do this, twice. He dozes with his enormous head in my arms and I lean against him. It's hard to know who's enjoying it more. People laugh at us. They clearly think I'm eccentric at best, crazy at worst. I don't really fit in at the yard. I'm twice as old as most people, three or four times the age of the swarms of pink-jodhpur-clad girls that inhabit the place on Saturdays. I don't like going fast. I lack confidence. I didn't ride from childhood. But here's the thing: I love this old cart horse and I don't care who knows it. So we stand in the shade, escaping the 80-degree heat, and hug each other. Slowly, a partnership is forming.

Back in the real world, something other-worldly is happening, and another partnership is about to be celebrated. Prince William is to marry his long-term sweetheart, Kate Middleton, giving every girl hope that one day her prince will come. The nation stops. Around the country there are more than 500 street parties as people use this as an excuse for a knees-up. But they'd be hard-pressed to beat ours.

Our road has always had a great sense of community. Back in the 1890s the railway ran along the bottom of the road, taking people to Alresford and Alton one way, and up to Winchester and thence to London the other. Forty-one railway workers' houses lined the road on two sides, with two larger ones at the top for the stationmaster and the signalman. But Dr Beeching closed the little line along with so many others in the 1960s, and the road became a dead end. You could quite happily live in this city for years and not know of its existence.

It lies on the edge of St Giles Hill, which in medieval times played host to the annual St Giles Fair, reputedly the greatest fair in Europe. It attracted traders from across Europe, bringing spices and silks from Asia, wine from Spain, textiles from Holland, and brass from Germany. There were jugglers and fire-eaters. Mystery plays were performed. The local taverns did very well. The last fair was held in 1834, but people of the parish of St John's still know how to throw a good party.

Because the road is in effect a Victorian cul-de-sac, there is no through traffic, and people stop to chat more. In one of these conversations, the idea of a Royal Wedding street party was born. Seven households did the heavy work, booking musicians, hiring trestle tables and chairs, crucially buying in an inordinate amount of alcohol, asking people to prepare cakes and salads, and planning a barbecue and games.

Miraculously, it comes together. On the eve of the party, the final shilly-shallyers come round with their financial contributions. The meat fills several fridges. Cakes have been made, glasses borrowed. A gazebo is put up to act as a bar. Someone writes a sign indicating that's what it is. Three of us go up and down the street putting the bunting up, while George-the-cat runs along behind trying to catch it. Everyone, obligingly, moves their cars out of the road to allow more room for jollity. At 11.40 p.m. when I finally crawl into bed, it's like the night before Christmas, with snow. Everything is silent, expectant, waiting for the morning.

The weather dawns fair, despite a forecast of heavy rain. We do watch the wedding, honest we do. (Pippa Middleton's bridesmaid's dress will live long in the memory.) But the bells peal and we pour out onto the street, fire up the barbecues, crack open the champagne, and party. Everyone is there from newborn babies to the elderly. My mother comes along as stand-in Queen. She is the closest we have to royalty. Phil gives her a plastic tiara, which she wears all day, including during a game of musical chairs. Her years spent teaching small children come into play at this point. She is the only adult left in the game with five chairs remaining, and wins a special prize and a huge round of applause.

There are more games involving (separately) toilet paper, water, flour, drinking, running, and general mess. Some kind soul has brought out a table-tennis table for the children, who are also enjoying the car-free day by running up and down, cycling, and drawing with chalk in the middle of the street. There is music, dancing, and far, far too much food and drink.

We'd worried that we had under-catered. Instead, we are sending people home with uncooked meat, bread rolls, and bags of crisps. George will live off the leftover cooked meat for days ahead. The four chickens that live in my back garden will be eating leftover salad until they are heartily sick of it. We are one barrel of locally produced beer over the required amount, so those with energy decamp to a neighbour's garden and carry on drinking all night. The remaining bottles of Pimm's will last several years, as Phil (who bought them) is keen to remind me.

My mother has arranged flowers on every trestle table. She smiles all day, drinks pots of tea, chats to all the neighbours, and looks much more relaxed and human than she has done for months, possibly years. I am cheered.

But the big star of the day is not my mother, despite the flowers she is given for being faux royalty. It is George. George was a rescue cat. I got him because he looked utterly ridiculous, with long fur, huge eyes, massive paws, and ears and a tail that would sit well on a squirrel. He also looked in dire need of love. He had clearly been beaten and abused, as well as abandoned. A kink in his tail suggests that, at one point, someone shut it in a door. It took eighteen months before he would come within arm's reach of me. But here he is at the street party, king of the road. It turns out he's now got over his fear and is incredibly sociable. He knows even more people than I do; certainly different people. Individuals that I've never met greet him by name and stroke him.

I'm flabbergasted. This is not a cat that wears a name collar. By the end of the evening it turns out that he regularly visits nineteen other houses – that's virtually half the street – for a chat and a stroke. The students who live two doors down the road tell me that they found him asleep in their wardrobe one day. Other people, on discovering that I'm George's owner, tell me that he calls in regularly and sleeps on their beds. Today is no exception for George's socializing. A rival party is under way in the next road; George slopes off to check it out. But he soon comes back. Our party is clearly the place to be on the day of the Royal Wedding, and he's not about to miss it. Other than the all-night drinkers, he is the last one to be hauled in to bed, protesting loudly as only a cat can.

May

Each summer, in August, the yard holds an open day. It's rather like a church fête, but with horses, and little attention paid to God. There is face painting for the children and the chance to have pony rides. There are a few stalls where you can buy things you don't need; plus tea, hot dogs, burgers, and cake. There's a raffle and music.

The big attraction, however, is the riding that goes on in the main arena. Generally, there is some in-hand showing, where you walk and trot round on foot with your horse and show off its movements to the judge. Anyone who doesn't ride would, at this stage, naturally say, "Surely you're missing something? Aren't you meant to be on top of that creature, not running beside it?" And when you are running around in the deep sand of the outdoor arena wearing your best horse-riding gear in warm sunshine, I tend to agree.

There are also ridden classes where you and your horse show off your moves in walk, trot, and canter. And, finally, there are two drill rides to music. The first is performed by customers, the second by the staff. The staff make it look easy. It isn't. I know this because Duke and I have been asked to take part in the customers' performance this year. We will be part of a team performing a routine in walk and trot to "Greased Lightning" from the film *Grease*. The number of things that can go wrong is so great that I don't know what to worry about first. Will I fall off? Will Duke be spooked by the loud music and bolt, turning the tune into reality? Will we, most likely of all, crash into another horse?

This is the top contender for Risk of The Day because we perform a figure of eight in trot, weaving in and out of each other as we reach the centre point of the eight. Annie and Kirsten are taking part too, which makes it more fun. But I am nonetheless daunted by the prospect. I am convinced that we will run into the side of another horse. It hasn't occurred to me yet that Duke won't want an accident, so will avoid the other horses at all costs, or that he is the head of the herd and so they will naturally avoid him, as this means they won't get an equine ticking off later.

Before our weeks of evening rehearsals start, Annie is practising alone in the outdoor school. She is working on her position in the saddle. This means doing some riding without stirrups. We all do this. Once you take your stirrups away, the theory goes, you use your muscles more: both your core muscles and those in your legs. It makes you sit deep in the saddle, think about your whole body, and rely far, far less on your feet and hands. This makes you ride better and consequently improves the way that your horse goes.

Duke and I often have lessons in the outdoor school, where we spend five or ten minutes working without stirrups in both walk and trot. At first it's unnerving, but it makes me concentrate, and, by the end of the lesson, I don't want to put my stirrups back and ride with them, because it's going so well.

It was probably like that for Annie, only she's more capable and can do this in canter too. So, during the practice session, she was riding without stirrups and coming back from canter to trot, slowing down around a bend. She lost her balance and fell sideways from Lady at some speed. Instinctively, she put her left arm down to break her fall. This is where things went very badly wrong. Jockeys are taught to roll when they fall rather than put their arms out, and I can now see why. Annie has broken her arm in five places.

Flick was watching and saw the accident. She ran over, caught the horse, and then told Annie to stay where she was, largely because she didn't want her to see the mess her arm was in, panic, and faint.

"But my arm hurts," said Annie.

"Not to worry," said Flick with huge presence of mind. "You've probably pulled a muscle." But she was looking at bones sticking out of Annie's arm as she spoke. An ambulance came. Hospital followed. Now Annie's arm is full of metal plates and bolts holding it all together. She has an angry red scar. She is shaken. We are all shaken. Annie and Lady are the steadiest, most positive horse-and-rider combination at the yard. If an accident can happen to them, it can happen to any of us, my worse self is keen to remind me. Horses are flight animals, and so there is always the risk of injury or of things not going to plan.

In the run-up to the 2012 Olympics, *Time* magazine asked if eventing was "the Olympics' most dangerous sport". In the eight years before the competition at Greenwich Park, some seven international riders had died whilst competing.

But you don't have to be a top eventer to suffer an injury. Things can go wrong when simply putting your horse out into the field, riding down a quiet country lane, or, as in Annie's case, practising in an arena, the place where you would normally feel at your most safe. Phil issues his regular warning about how completely hazardous this all is, but knows that I am unlikely to give up now that I've caught the equine bug.

The customer team for the open day is all a-jitter. Individually, we are practising hard, booking the arena to rehearse the performance again and again. We're all taking lessons too in order to try to overcome our weaknesses. As I have many of those, I book some lessons with Flick as we build towards the big day, which, as yet, is a few months off. Just like Annie, this means working on my position. I too will have to take my feet out of the stirrups and ride in the school. I know where she fell. When we go past the spot, I find myself looking down at the sand as if daring it to rise up and cause me injury too, checking for bloodstains. It is, for many of us now, the scary corner of the arena.

Riding without stirrups requires all my concentration at the best of times. I have to relax – not currently my strong suit – sit deep, breathe, and engage all my muscles to work at one with Duke, to guide, encourage, and go with his movement. Riding like this, remembering what has happened to my pal, has my nerves jangling. So Flick ups the difficulty level to force me to think about myself, not Annie. I'm to do rising trot without stirrups. I wonder if this is humanly possible. Every stride that Duke takes I have to rise and sit without having stirrups to push myself up. I'm going to have to lift myself up whilst keeping my lower leg still and solid.

I don't think I can do it. But as this is the road to certain failure, I imagine what it would be like to be able to do it, and then, as if by magic, find myself going round the arena moving up and down as if I had stirrups – when I don't. I am delighted. Even Flick, whose standards are very high, is pleased. Duke knows he's earned some carrots and takes great delight in eating them and then dozing off while I groom him at the end of our session.

It's a much-needed encouragement, as, back in the haunted part of my life, the time has now come to find a permanent care home for my father. Social services gives us a list of local options, some of which aren't very local and take nearly an hour to reach by car. We book appointments at four and head off round the county.

It is a horrible shock. The homes are full of old people with dementia. Of course they are; these are homes that care for old, demented people. My father too is elderly and has dementia. But somehow I haven't caught up with the idea that this is the reality, and it is going to get worse. Suddenly, as we walk around the first two homes, I come face to face with what my father will look like, and I don't want to see it. That's the odd thing about dementia. You never quite keep up with what is happening.

Everyone's experience of dementia is different, of course, but very often the person concerned will stay on a level for some time and then have a marked decline, followed by another plateau, and so it goes on. I never come to terms with my father's declines. I'll just about have acclimatized myself to one set of changes when another comes along, and I'm left behind again. This is made all the worse by the fact that he still looks like himself. So every day I am duped into thinking that he is the person he always was: the man who taught me to love cricket; adored *To Kill a Mockingbird*; read me Chaucer as a bedtime story when I was a small child; and made daft rhymes out of biblical texts.

The first home is set in beautiful Hampshire countryside. There is even a dark bay horse grazing in a paddock next door. I think it must be a good omen. It isn't. The manager shows us around. Huge, cavernous rooms are full of people whose wits have left them. They stare vacantly into space. Some dribble. Some have stains on their clothes. They all have that dressed-by-a-carer look about them. Their bodies are present, but their spirits have already left the building. Despite a number of strategically placed toilets, there is an all-pervasive smell of urine: the aroma, I will come to discover in a few years' time, of the end days of dementia.

My mother and I are so horrified that we can neither look at each other nor speak. We trail around after the manager, nod as he explains things, and then walk away. It is like looking into the abyss. The second home is in a town at the far end of the county.

It's on a busy dual carriageway, and it's not a pleasant drive. This puts us both off before we even get through the door. This home is more modern than the first, but there is still a persistent smell of urine. Desperate, hollow-eyed relatives sit around with their family members, unable to make conversation.

The third home is very near my parents' house. I could walk there across the fields and it would be a short drive for my mother. It is hot as fire inside, as the heating is turned up to keep the residents warm. But the deciding factor against home number three is the day room. Thirteen women sit silently in chairs positioned round the walls. There is one spare chair, for my father. This would never do.

So to home number four. I remember little about this one except that it is low-ceilinged and dark and has the air of a run-down school outbuilding. You wouldn't leave a dog you didn't like here – and I like virtually all dogs – let alone your father.

The trawl round the county has revealed two things. First, we have little choice because our room will be paid for by a combination of social services and Daddy's accumulated pensions. This is because the family income is insufficient to warrant a private room. Later, I'll realize that this is a good thing. You can shed your life savings, or have to sell your home to meet care costs. Fortunately, that is not our position. But right now I'm only struck by the restrictions, not the benefits, of our situation.

On average, you can expect to pay £27,200 a year in residential costs. This can go up by another £10,000 if nursing care is needed, as it will one day be. However, in the south of England, some residential care homes charge more than £40,000 a year. This is more than it costs to send a child to Eton. Not many of us can choose to do that. We don't have any option when it comes to our parents. An extremely kind, sympathetic woman is sent from the council to go through our finances with a fine-tooth comb and assess what we can pay. She does this with such care and compassion that we want to hug her. But it doesn't get away from the fact that our lack of financial clout means that Daddy has fewer options. You are poor, so your dad gets a rubbish room. That seems to be the silent, take-away message.

I take this particularly hard because, right now, money is tight. Freelance journalists don't normally wash themselves in five-pound notes, with a few honourable exceptions. But I've always managed to make ends meet. The recession has hit the newspaper industry hard, and, being the most expendable, freelancers like me are losing work. Rates too are plummeting. And it's been known for payments never to arrive. Staff journalists are also taking on a different attitude, seemingly resentful of the idea of paying others when they themselves expect to be paid. "We don't pay freelancers" is an oft-heard mantra.

"I do this for a living, just like you," I say. They shrug.

I've always been busy, but now, during the recession, the phone doesn't ring as much and my income is down by a third. I'm living off my dwindling savings. So I can't turn round and fish money out of an account to make my father's last years more comfortable, and this stings. It's bad enough feeling that your career is on hold because of bankers' greed. It's worse when this means you can't help your parents. On the news, banking leaders are still busy saying that the recession isn't their fault. I'd like them to come and meet my father, see the rooms in these four care homes, and let me explain to them the unintended consequence of their actions.

So the gloomy tour of the county has revealed our not-so-genteel poverty when it comes to affording eye-watering care fees. It's also revealed what the future will be for my dad. One day he will become one of those elderly people that we saw sitting silently in chairs waiting to die. He will outlive his body and his mind. He will lose the power of speech. He will be unable to stand or walk without a team of people helping him. He won't be able to dress himself, or wash. He will need help eating meals. He won't be able to read or write. And, worst of all, he will become doubly incontinent.

I rage against this. I want it to stop. I want to draw out a magic wand, like Hermione Granger in the *Harry Potter* novels, and freeze my father's condition in the not-so-great state that it is now. This, I figure, is bad enough. How can it possibly get worse? But it will. A friend of mine saw her aunt decline and fade with dementia. She works in the health service and tells me how it will be, even though I don't want to know. When I complain that it's bad now, she says it will be worse. She's right, of course.

Losing someone to dementia is a daily grief. Unlike losing someone suddenly, which would be bad enough, each day you are bereaved by degrees. And this goes on for years, whilst all around you friends are marrying, having children, and getting new jobs and bigger houses. Inside, I am uttering a long, silent scream. One particular moment stands out for me. It was the day that my father couldn't carve Sunday lunch. He had always been, I think it's fair to say, useless around the house. He'd been brought up to be; his mother did everything for him. But he prided himself on always carving the Sunday roast, and always washing up. His washing up had, for some years, been getting increasingly bad. He couldn't see the food that needed to be washed off and wasn't sure what he was doing. But it could all be done again quietly later, when he wasn't looking.

Then, on this particular Sunday, he hovered in the kitchen unsure what to do. "You could carve the chicken," I said, because he always did that. He looked at me, frightened and mystified, glancing from the knife to the chicken as if he simply had no idea what I was talking about.

"I've never done that before," he said. "I don't know how to do it." I fell through an emotional trap door as the dementia chipped away at who he had been and what he could do.

Yet the unpalatable truth was that he was going to decline. There would be more chicken-carving moments, more steps down the ladder of infirmity. There is one this month. I go to visit my father after work. He tells me that it saddens him to lose his memory.

"I know your name is Hazel," he says, "but not much else." *Soon that too will be gone*, I think. I don't expect it to happen as fast as it does. After I leave, he rings my mother. "I had a visit from that lady," he says.

"What lady?" she asks.

"That cousin of yours," he says, hoping he's right. But it was me, his only daughter. A home has to be found, and we are doing it against the clock.

So my mother starts to ask around among her friends for advice: who knows any good care homes? One friend from church pops round with a brochure that covers the whole county. We see places here that we haven't heard of and start to ring round. Many are full. Many more haven't got a bed for someone on social services rates, which are considerably lower than private ones. We are essentially waiting for someone in a social services bed to die so that we can re-house my father and ensure that my mother lives. It is quite awful.

Our search takes us to a small, county town about ten miles away. On its outskirts is a modern care home that is divided into sections: we'll call them elderly, slightly demented, really demented, and very nearly dead. This means that my father wouldn't be with people in a more advanced state than he is, which has to be positive. Everything is glistening, clean, and new.

There is one upstairs room on a social services level that he could have. It has a bed, an armchair, a wardrobe, a chest of drawers, a table, and a basin. The toilet is just across the corridor. It's a bright, cheerful room.

"And", says Dave, the care worker charged with showing us around, "can you smell anything?" We are mystified. What does he mean?

"There is no smell of urine," he says. And there isn't. We practically fall on his neck with relief. The staff are kind and friendly. There are activities for the more able. The menu looks reasonable. And, most importantly, it doesn't smell.

I feel as if we've hauled ourselves over an invisible finishing line. But we haven't. I ring the social work team to say that we've found a great place and would love my father to go there. Naïvely, I'm expecting this to be well received. We have, after all, been using our weekends to drive round the county identifying somewhere for him to live, and have found a place within the allotted time. It doesn't turn out like this. "No," says the social worker. "He can't go there. His needs are too severe. That care home has turned him down." I feel as if I'm in an out-of-control lift plummeting towards the ground floor. Everything is shooting past me and I can barely breathe.

"They can't have turned him down," I say. "They said they'd be happy to have him."

So begin twenty-four hours of Chinese Whispers in which it's hard to work out who is really saying what. The social worker stands her ground. I stand mine. I am at the railway station in rush hour when this happens, surrounded by fellow commuters. I go bounding over the social etiquette of how to use phones in public places and virtually have a stand-up row with the social worker. Never mind saying "I'm on the train"; I am vitriolic. Having found somewhere that is odour-free for my dad, I will not be forced to leave him somewhere I consider to be wretched because of bureaucracy. I am fighting with every fibre of my being. Everyone on the station platform is very British and pretends (and no doubt wishes) that I am not shouting and am not there.

My normally polite, courteous mother follows this up by ringing social services and completely losing her temper – something that I've never seen happen before. The result of all this is that my father will be assessed for suitability for the care home in a few days' time. But you shouldn't have to shout to make this happen, should you? I crawl into bed at 8 p.m. and cry myself to sleep. Only, of course, I don't sleep. I have psychedelic nightmares and spend most of the night with my head in my hands, curled up in a ball. This goes on for several days and interminable nights.

The day of the meeting to discuss this dawns. I've had no more than three hours' sleep every night all week. I am braced for the worst. I am ready for more arguments. But in the ebb and flow of this hall-of-mirrors experience, the tide has unexpectedly gone out, taking with it all risk of the unpalatable. My father is to go to the sweetly-scented care home permanently. My mother will have the chance to recover from her stroke. Relief washes over me. My father takes a different view. He is implacably opposed to the move. He'll be going home in a few days, he tells me. He is not going anywhere else. I haven't the strength to argue. The sunny upstairs room will be his.

Phil calls today "Collapse In A Heap Day". This is all I can do after months of not sleeping, worry, and uncertainty. We have a result. We have a pleasant home for Daddy to live in. We are on the cusp of something new. But I am so weary that I can barely speak. I've certainly lost the ability to write, which is fairly serious if you're a journalist. I've only had writer's block once before, nearly twenty years ago, after my first foreign assignment left me traumatized and sick from the after-effects of taking Lariam, an anti-malarial medication. For six months then, I felt as if I was hanging on to my sanity by my fingernails. The words stopped flowing. Now they've stopped once more.

I understand it this time. My mind has had enough. It hasn't currently got the capacity to be creative. I stare at a blank screen every day. Nothing happens. This is such a contrast to normal as to be an out-of-body experience. As a rule, I am permanently writing copy in my head. As I interview people, I'm looking for The Moment, the point at which I know the story will start, when put down in words. As I drive, do the washing up, go shopping, paragraphs of text are writing and rewriting themselves in my head. The words are a constant, self-polishing torrent that never dries up. I go to bed mentally writing copy. I awake with words forming themselves into fresh paragraphs. Only now there isn't even a trickle. I haven't written for days. I can't imagine words ever coming out of my fingers again. Today, the sofa is the place for me. I lie there and feel like a dog that's been kicked nearly to death. Every part of my body hurts. My mind, soul, and spirit hurt too. I am bruised and wounded.

Nonetheless, I do have to go on working somehow, as there are stories to be told. I am going through the motions when I interview the Archbishop of Canterbury, and then fly to Edinburgh to do a series of features. I'm asking the right questions, but my heart isn't engaged in it. I don't much care what anyone says. I wouldn't recognize a great story now if it leapt out at me. I'm researching stories for national newspapers. Things are being published. But it could be happening to someone else; I feel distant from all of it. My diary is an endless to-do list: work, come home, feed the cat and hens, check both parents are alive, make time to really listen to both of them, prepare sandwiches for the next day, go to bed, fail to sleep. Repeat for five days. At the weekend, there are a few variants: buy food, wash clothes, do any admin (mine, Mummy's, Daddy's), ride Duke, go to church, visit both parents.

My social life has evaporated. I remember, a few years ago, someone telling me that they'd lost all their friends when their father developed dementia. I couldn't understand it. How could you lose all your friends? How careless. Now I know what it's like. You don't have the time or energy to phone or visit people. They too are busy and so don't phone or visit you. Plus, everyone knows that Daddy has dementia. It's like a death: no one knows what to say or do. So the simplest thing to do is not ask. And the easiest way not to ask is not to phone. A few friends still ring up for a chat. I try not to tell them what's happening, not wanting to become The Person Who Always Moans. These are stalwart buddies who've been around for decades. I appreciate their calls beyond measure, even if I can't express it. But many precious friendships have faded through lack of care, time, and attention. At a time when I could really do with friends to prop me up, I find that I have fewer than I had expected.

Going to the yard is my one escape. I find myself, unexpectedly, looking forward to the drill ride on open day. Despite its terrors, it gives me something to focus on. However, our after-work practices are not going well. For several weeks we have been crashing into each other as we mistime cross-overs, and then we sit on our bemused horses, laughing amid the pandemonium. It's only a five-minute routine, but we always forget it. Each week, every one of us will forget something, causing the whole thing to descend into chaos. We all shout instructions to each other. The instructors shout directions. We are a noisy, but rather jolly, mess.

Annie's husband brings her along to watch. She is white with pain. Her normally cheerful demeanour has rubbed very thin. She smiles and watches for a while, but leaves early. She is not strong enough to be out of the house for long, and it must be dreadfully sad to watch someone else ride Lady, knowing that she is unlikely to be fit to ride when the open day comes round.

Duke and I chug along in trot, falling behind the others' pace, causing asymmetry in the performance, and threatening crashes. "Go faster, Hazel," Flick says every week.

"I can't go any faster," I say, puffing and genuinely believing that it is impossible for a horse to go faster than this steady plod. Have I not watched any horse racing? Have I not heard of galloping?

"Yes, you can," she responds every time. I am not sure how you make three-quarters of a tonne of horse go faster without hitting it with a whip, which I don't want to do. No one, I reckon, ever found a beating encouraging. Though this isn't quite the same thing, I feel sure there has to be another way, if only I could discover it.

The answer is, apparently, to rise out of the saddle more quickly. You set the pace of the horse by the speed at which you rise in trot, backing it up with energy from your legs cranked onto his sides. We try this, with me thinking that, quite frankly, it isn't going to work. But of course it does. Duke speeds up. We catch up with our section of the ride. We will not cause crashes if we go on like this. This represents progress. But I'm not going to be winning medals any time soon.

However lacklustre my performance, the staff know that Duke understands his job and will turn in a good show on the day. Accordingly, they place him at the lead of one of the two strings of horses when we divide to go round the arena. This requires me not only to steer Duke accurately, remember the whole test so that I can lead everyone round, and rise out of the saddle fast enough to set a decent pace, but also to stay level with another horse and rider on the opposite side of the school. You have to be kidding. The best I can say each week is, "I only went wrong once." I am not setting a shining example of how to do a drill ride. In order not to shame myself, Duke, the drill ride, and the whole yard, Flick suggests that I practise at home, *sans* horse.

I draw the letters that mark any dressage arena on pieces of paper: A K V E S H, C M R B P F and, for the purposes of this test, also Q. Who makes this stuff up? What's wrong with the alphabet in order? Anyway, that is not my concern. I stick them round the kitchen and every night practise the routine, its bends, turns, half-circles, full circles, serpentines, halts, and the dreaded figures of eight. I practise walking, trotting, halting. I have become one of the little girls at my school who trotted round the playground. George-the-cat stares at me in disbelief. I can't quite believe it either. I am a middle-aged journalist who is spending what we will laughingly call her spare time trotting round the kitchen, halting at the old wicker chair and the big food cupboard, walking past the oven, circling by the sink, bowing in the middle of the room. And this is relaxation? Heaven save me. Things must be even worse than I thought they were.

June

Athletes say that, in a race, you have to keep running when you are exhausted and everything hurts. Profoundly. The difference between winning the race and coming second or third is your ability to hold your form and keep powering towards the line, rather than faltering because you are spent. We seldom see athletes being stretchered off the track after a race, but sometimes we do, when the whole thing has taken too much out of them even if they have won. They have simply run themselves into the ground.

I'm starting to feel like that. I imagine myself to be a 400-metre runner who's done 300 metres and hasn't got enough left in the tank for that last dash for the line. But strength, resilience, and endurance will have to be found to get through this last little bit: settling my father into the sweet-smelling care home. Of course, what I haven't realized is that, actually, I'm required to be a marathon runner, not a distance sprinter. We may be six years into our own particular experience of dementia, but we have many, many more miles ahead. The bell is not going to ring as I do this particular lap that is consuming my waking and sleeping thoughts. It's a good job I don't realize that right now.

If one of your relatives is diagnosed with dementia, and joins the more than three-quarters of a million Britons with the condition, my advice would be to take one day at a time. Worrying about the future gets you nowhere. It eats your strength. An awful range of spectres haunt you. They haunt me now. I am signally failing to live a day at a time. But with the day of the big move pending, my mother and I go to the new care home to make Daddy's room... well, a bit more homely. I've had his two favourite pictures reframed: one of black-backed gulls on a sea wall, the other a drawing of his uncle at work in his outhouse.

My great-uncle was one of the last of the bodgers. A "bodge job" is generally taken to mean a poor job, a mess. But bodgers like my great-uncle were in fact highly skilled craftsmen, making chair legs by hand on pole lathes. My great-uncle and his father made chair legs from cherry wood in a workshop that abutted their village-end home. These were sold to the local chair-making industry. The workshop was an extraordinary place, full of movement and beauty, but also fantastically messy. I don't think it had ever been swept out, resulting in billowing waves of wood shavings that reached high up the walls.

One day, the story goes, an artist was passing the workshop (this being a time when people walked rather than drove) and asked if he could sketch my great-uncle as he made the chair legs. This picture is the result. It's always hung in my parents' house and is a reminder of far-off childhood days that are still dimly there in my father's memory. He tells me that he can remember watching football matches on the village common when he was four years old. After that, there's blankness.

We take cushions, his radio, his much-thumbed Bible, birdwatching books and binoculars, tins of biscuits, clothes, shoes, even a coat (which he will never wear again) and a wash bag. It's not much to be left with at the end of eighty years, but it does succeed in making the room more personal. We are, we will realize much, much later, utterly kidding ourselves that he'll be able to read the Bible, look at the books, think of looking out of the window at birds, or remember that there are biscuits to be eaten. It would be worse if we knew this.

The care home manager has put a picture of a lapwing on

my dad's bedroom door, as this is one of his most-beloved birds from a life of birdwatching. She hopes it will help him to identify this as his room. Then we go home and wait for time to pass, as it inevitably must. I know I can't take my dad from one care home to the other. First, I'll feel yet again that I am abandoning him, but this time for good. Second, he will be distressed and rage against me the whole way, asking to go home. My nerves aren't up to the job; I am too much of a coward for this task.

So I turn to Barry, a quietly-spoken care worker who has been our guardian angel for the last six years. His role has been to support my dad rather than us and he's done that with aplomb, providing reassurance, encouragement, understanding, and, more than anything else, a listening ear, in the many times when my father couldn't make sense of what was going on. In doing so he has become the brother I never had. I am utterly sure that I wouldn't have a shred of sanity at this point if it hadn't been for Barry. He has stood beside me shoulder to shoulder and now I need his help one last time. He is to take Daddy to the care home that he will leave only in death.

I feel sick and numb all day, wondering how it's going, imagining terrible scenes, feeling like Judas. Then Barry phones and says that, honestly, it went fine. Not to worry. He is of course paid to say this. Nonetheless, I choose to believe him and am both relieved and grateful. There have been times over the last three months when I thought we'd never get to this point, and far more times when I never wanted us to. I do not want this to be true. I do not want to put my father into care.

People's reactions to what's happening are intriguing. A few people – my dearest friends and some wise, insightful souls – say that this is the best thing that can be done in such an awful situation. This will keep Mervyn safe, they say. It is for his benefit. He won't find the car keys and drive off, or fall down the stairs, or any other terrifying thing. He will be with trained professionals who know how to cope with his dementia and can take care of him properly.

But most people don't react like that. I can see them thinking that they would never do this to their parents; that it is a betrayal; that I quite clearly don't care, or, if I do care, then I do so more about myself than for my dad. I've stopped telling people what's going on because I haven't the energy to deal with the judgment that passes over their faces, that is built in to their body language, that is spoken or unspoken, left hanging in the air. Yet I sympathize with their position. I would have felt like that myself. I would never have imagined that I would do this. It does feel like a betrayal. I am judging myself every day, and I do not come off well out of that judgment. But then I look at my mother and know that I have to do this. It is a choice forged in hell.

The kindly care home manager advises us not to come for a few days. She doesn't say that this is because these days will be turbulent, that my dad will be raging against staying there, that the whole thing will be dreadfully upsetting. But that's what she means. It's not like this for everyone. Some people settle well. Others welcome the security of a care home. But throughout his dementia, my father has had absolutely no insight into his condition. He thinks we're all lying, that this is some terrible conspiracy against him, that I particularly have left him and walked away. No wonder he's angry and upset. So, after a few days in which we hope the emotional dust will have settled, my mother and I visit.

It is beyond awful. Daddy has been sedated, which I'd expected, simply to calm his nerves. But with sedation goes personality. He looks like an old, crumpled blob of a man, not my proud, intelligent, somewhat stroppy father. He is bent over in his chair, dribbling, eyes watering, struggling for words. When he can talk, he asks endlessly about coming home. How long will he be here? He won't be here for ever, will he? We don't answer. We've been advised not to. Wait, says Barry. Tell him in a few months' time. It will be easier then. If I got down on my stomach and slithered through the grass, I would not feel more like a serpent than I already do.

This whole experience has been marked by things that I have not wanted to do: put him into temporary care, now permanent care, and, as if anything could be worse, take out what's called a Deprivation of Liberty Order. It does what it says on the tin. It means that my dad can't leave full-time care. I've hemmed him in legally. Here he will stay despite the fact that he hates it and doesn't understand it. Then I have to smile, hold his hand, and explain that all these hateful things have been done because I love him and want the best for him. It sounds like a lie to me. It really sounds like a lie to him.

I'm presuming that it also sounds like a lie to a lot of people I know. I'm learning (slowly) not to respond to people's need to hear me say that Daddy will get better. It's crazy. But this is clearly what a lot of people want. "How's your dad?" they ask, giving me a look that I recognize means "Tell me he's OK, doing well". No one wants to hear the truth, so I don't tell it. But in the fullness of time, I will start telling the truth. "He can't walk, can't stand, can't talk much, and is doubly incontinent," I'll end up saying. "Oh dear," people will say. "I didn't realize he was that bad. Hopefully he'll soon be well." "Dementia", I will say, "is not something from which you get better." People don't like that. The truth. But I will become sick of lying, sick of putting on a brave face. My brave face will have melted away.

Perhaps it's no surprise, therefore, that I wake the day after all this feeling an unfamiliar emotion. I sort through the emotions that I know well and don't recognize it. I lie in bed considering what it might be. Finally, it dawns on me that it is depression. I have been so consumed by what's been happening in my family for the last six months – well, six years – that everything else has been on hold. I feel, as I lie in bed putting off the moment when I must get up, that my career is behind me, that I'll never do any interesting assignments again. How can I when my brain is addled and I don't even want to get up in the morning? In June, when the world is at its most beautiful. I feel as if fun, laughter, lightness of spirit, and happiness have all gone for ever. I am left with a leaden feeling in my body and spirit. I don't feel like myself any more. I am an athlete with no more strength to finish the race. If I could stay in bed for ever and refuse to face the day, I would.

But I can't. There is a large black horse that is expecting my presence at the yard. He'll be looking at his watch, I tell myself, and drag myself out of bed and out of the house. Daddy used to say this about the cat and the chickens. Now I say it. It created order in the day for him, and now it is doing so for me: caring for this horse beats all other known cures for sadness.

In January, let's be honest, Duke would have preferred me not to be riding him, let alone picking out his hooves and trying to get the tangles out of his nearly floor-length tail. And, at the start, I had rather wished I wasn't riding him either. He was too tall, too strong. I was fearful, and he knew it. But imperceptibly things have changed. Now, six months on, when I walk into the yard he recognizes my footfall and the jangle of the new red head collar that I've bought him, and pokes his head over the stable door, ears pricked. "Ah, it's you," his body language seems to be saying. "What are we going to get up to today?" Yes, this massive horse seems to be viewing us as a team. And I definitely am. The yard is blessed with a wide range of ponies and horses, all with different personalities, many of them far more conventionally sleek and attractive than Duke. But I have eyes for none of them. It's Duke that I love.

Yes, though I am still a bit scared, I truly love this old horse. Formerly, I would have thought this impossible. Next, you'll be telling me that I'll acquire a late-in-life fondness for large spiders or venomous snakes. So it is with some relief that I walk into the yard and see two dark ears pricked, two dark, mournful eyes questioning. Today we are having yet another lesson, in a bid to improve our halt-to-trot transitions before the big day dawns and we must perform in front of the open-day crowds. Duke's had a day off, which has done him a power of good, and he is on a mission, trotting into the school full of energy. Flick and I wonder if we've got the right horse, as Duke prefers a steady hack round the woods to the equine equivalent of musical scales practice in the arena any day of the week.

But it bodes well for working on our transitions. This is just a fancy name for going from one speed to another. To do this well you must have your horse sufficiently engaged and listening to you, in order to move smoothly from one to the next. Believe me when I say that it doesn't just happen. When you watch a rider making a transition, let's say from walk to trot, look smooth, effortless, and silky, they are in fact putting in considerable effort. Walk-to-trot we can do. Halt-to-trot requires a whole load more engagement, listening, and energy than either of us has been deploying. This, let it be said, is entirely my fault. Duke can do it. I'm just not giving him the right signals to get him to do it. I must squeeze with my legs, whilst allowing him to move forward with my hands. I must mean it. But I must do this so subtly that no one except Duke knows I'm asking him to move. There are to be no Pony Club kicks. Whilst effective, they look messy and are unnecessary and, I think, unkind. If I were Duke, I would not want to be kicked in the sides. I'd rather be asked politely.

So we work on polite-but-firmness, going up and down through different gaits until I'm doing it smoothly and Duke is responding well. Then we halt, as we will have to in the middle of the drill ride, count to ten, and then I squeeze-and-allow, and Duke springs into trot. Well, when I say "springs", that might be a bit of journalistic licence. But it was definitely a trot. We do it again and again. Greased lightning it isn't. Trot it is. If I can remember the routine, there is now every chance that we won't disgrace ourselves on the open day. I am very pleased.

Probably, part of the satisfaction in achieving a halt-to-trot transition (something I'd not heard of six months ago) is simply that it is an attainable goal. It is something that, with work, I can do. There is, right now, so much that I can't do. I can't stop my father slipping away into the mists of dementia. I can't heal my mother's frazzled nervous system or stroke-damaged heart. I can't stop either of them from dying. It is a daily nightmare that I don't lose when I sleep and which is still there in the morning, endlessly. So walk-to-trot represents a tangible result.

It's been decided that my mother is well enough to manage for a few days, so Phil and I hop on a plane and head to the Isle of Skye for a three-day culinary tour. Western Scotland is renowned for its high-quality local produce, and, being fans of this (wherever it is found), we are keen to spend a few days, well… eating, basically. That is pretty much all we do for three days, except laugh. We laugh almost from the moment that breakfast is finished (it's too early to laugh before we've eaten) until bedtime, which in Scotland in midsummer is pretty late. We are laughing so hard between courses at the world-famous Three Chimneys restaurant that the waiter thinks better of interrupting the hilarity with the next part of the meal and retreats, walking backwards slightly nervously, keeping an eye on us and making no sudden, sharp movements. People don't laugh like that at The Three Chimneys, obviously. There is a pause in the merriment for a fabulously good cheeseboard with home-made oatcakes that will live long in the memory, and then off we go again, laughing some more. It is even more of a tonic than the clean Scottish air and the ridiculously good food.

By the end of day three, I think that if anyone offers me any more seafood I might weep. We have completely and utterly overdone it. We have pole-vaulted into unnecessary amounts of food and we have had a blast. On the last day we head to the Loch Leven Seafood Café, which is reputedly the best seafood restaurant in the whole of Scotland, and that really is saying something. Whoever said this was not wrong. Forgetting our previous indulgences for a moment, we settle on the shellfish platter, which, when it arrives, appears to have been served in a dustbin lid, the portion is so huge. There is a lobster and a crab, mussels, cockles, razor clams, scallops, and oysters. It is sensational and far, far too much. After what seems like the entire night I grind to a halt and can eat no more, whimpering when offered one last razor clam. Phil keeps going, but even he is beaten in the end.

We were the first diners to arrive, so everyone else sees what we're eating and (with the exception of two sets of people who have the wisdom to choose something a mite more realistic) orders it too. Soon the whole restaurant is tucking into far, far too much shellfish. It's a bad night to be a clam in Loch Leven. It's a good night to be us.

But the oddest thing happens to me. Normally, this would be more than enough. I'd be concentrating on good company and equally good food. Instead, I look into the gloaming and think, *It's light enough still to be riding. I wish Duke was here. We could go for a late-evening hack. That would be the perfect end to the day.* And I find myself wondering if the real Hazel Southam has been captured by aliens and replaced by someone who looks similar but is unrecognizable. I am missing a horse on my three days of holiday. I'd better not tell anyone, or there will be grave concerns for my sanity.

Back at home, refreshed, brighter, smiling, I face the daunting task of telling my dad that, no, he isn't coming home. Not now. Not ever. Sorry. I visit him as soon as I'm back and find that he has packed all his clothes and possessions into the dirty linen box, in lieu of a suitcase. Then he has forgotten that he's done this and is worried that things are going missing. I pretend it's quite normal to pack your dirty linen box with books, socks, and so forth, and quietly put them all back, whilst chatting lightly.

Then I sit down and tell him the truth. This is his home now. He's not well enough to come home. And he won't be getting better. This team of carers can look after him properly and we simply can't. I am very, very sorry. He looks me in the eye and understands. We hold hands and cry. He never cries. We have the kind of conversation that you have before someone dies. We talk of love and laughter, God, cats, *The Guardian*, and cricket. I remind him of the village where we all grew up, of its orchards, his football team. He asks "Where do I live?" and "Where is my house?" a great deal these days. I used to try explaining, but as none of it makes any sense to him – the last seventy-five years having been wiped out – I talk about the village instead. That, he remembers.

I feel, as my mother often says, like a wrung-out piece of rag. There are things that you don't want to tell your parents: my A-Level results aren't very good; I've left my job with the big publishing company; I'll be reporting from a war zone. But "You're not coming home" is by far the worst. I comfort myself with the thought that, however bleak this moment, it won't come again. Daddy knows now and, whilst we may discuss it in the future, it won't be like this. Only, of course, it is. The next day and the day after and every day for years he will ask when he's coming home and I will have to tell him the freshly shocking news that he won't be. Every time it will be new to him, as five minutes later he will have forgotten it entirely. It is my own personal hell, and his too probably.

When I was starting out in journalism, wet behind the ears and hopelessly wide-eyed, there were times when I found the living-in-London-trying-to-prove-myself lark, well, not very larkish. At those times, my mother's homespun advice was to "smell something lovely; look at something lovely; taste something lovely; touch something lovely; and listen to something lovely every day". It was advice based on the dual principles of slowing down and gaining perspective by concentrating on something other than yourself.

It works, of course. Now it sounds like mindfulness, the latest trend in slowing-down-and-shutting-up-that-we-can't-call-prayer-in-case-someone-thinks-we're-religious. But then, it was just my mum's advice, and I followed it, smelling flowers, looking at the clouds, savouring a cup of tea, stroking the cat, and so on. Now, I can satisfy nearly all five senses with just one visit to Duke. So I find myself, one evening after drill practice, walking up to the fields behind the yard with two other girls, leading the horses to their night-time quarters. The sky is that blueish-pinky-mauve that sums up England in midsummer and is, without doubt, my favourite colour. The light is caught somewhere between the slowly setting sun and an enormous, rising harvest moon. The wayside violets are closing their petals. Late-in-the-day swallows swoop and dive around us, even skimming through the horses' legs as we trudge slowly up the steep slope towards the fields.

Swallows love farmland, where there is a good supply of both insects and water. With water troughs for the horses and a constant amount of poo being produced, the yard is perfect for the swallows. They nest in a building that we all call "the canopy": a long open-ended barn with stalls along both sides. It is here that the horses rest during the day between rides. The rafters are home to the swallows, which arrived this year on 14 April. They had flown all the way from their winter home in South Africa, across the Sahara – let's think about that: a tiny bird flying at 17–22 mph across the Sahara Desert – and then on up through Morocco, Spain, and France, and finally over the Channel, back to the yard where they were born, and to which they will always return. It is quite extraordinary and every year I cheer when I see their glossy blue-black backs swooping through the canopy and up onto a beam.

They are flying tonight to catch the rich supply of insects that dance on the still, summer-evening air. Swallows surround us. They are underneath us, flitting past on all sides, swirling above our heads, and, in the fields beyond, we can see them skimming the top of the long grass for insects that have danced their last in the yellowish air. It is quiet, so quiet, with just the sound of three sets of heavy hooves plodding up the track. My spirit soars with the swallows. Not everything is bleak, after all. I am looking at something beautiful, listening to something beautiful, touching something beautiful as I stroke Duke's back, and smelling that heady aroma of warm horse. All that's left is to taste something wonderful, and over the past few days I've done quite enough of that.

July

Increasingly, I find that I have the courage to ride out with Duke alone. But not always. There are days when I know deep in my soul that I am not a horse rider. I am just a journalist sitting on a horse, which is a very different thing. I fret about it at night, as light relief from worrying about my parents. What I fear is not necessarily what Duke will do in any given circumstance, but how I will react. I will freeze with fear. I am not a leader. I am not a rider. I am not selling anything to my horse. I shouldn't be riding at all, says my worse self. What's wrong with aerobics? Quite a lot, says my right knee, which is weakened by more than twenty years of aerobics classes. On days like this, I get myself into such a near-death tizzy that I will not allow myself to ride, and I simply groom Duke instead. No one at the yard understands this. They may sympathize, but they think I'm crazy. They all want to ride all day and every day. I have to summon every fibre of my being to do it.

Why is this? Years earlier on this mad caper of a bid to learn to ride, I was doing so at a small yard in a neighbouring village. It was delightful. The people were friendly and patient. One day, we went for a long ride that was fraught from the word go. We rode round the village collecting small children on ponies as we went, which is surely a hazardous occupation in itself. Then we headed out through the fields to find that, as it was after 12 August, the shooting season had begun, and a shoot was taking place right over our heads. Horses do not like this, let me tell you. Neither did I. There is a reason why guns are used to start races. There was considerable leaping about, skittish behaviour, and trying to run for home – and that was just the people. I jest. I was sent out in front because we were coming to a fast road and we all needed to stop, or face certain death. So I was the stopping point. We got over the road and went round the woods at some speed, with my nerve by now completely lost. On the route back, some of the horses shied at new markings on the road before we crossed over the fast main road again.

We were nearly home, but tired and jittery, when it happened. There was only about 100 yards to go. We turned into the narrow lane that led to the stables just as a massive combine harvester came the other way, blocking the road. The first rider took himself out of harm's way up onto the cricket pitch that ran alongside the road. I came next. I knew my pony was fine with combine harvesters. So what should I do: follow the first horse, or walk on the road past the machine? That moment's indecision and basic error of judgment on my part cost us all dear. The lead horse couldn't work out where his friends were, threw his rider onto the cricket pitch, and bolted for home along the road. My pony – who had a background in endurance riding, which is marathon riding for horses, and could therefore go all day – thought that this was a sign of trouble and went after him.

I was insufficiently experienced to be able to stop him. So we flew down the road towards the stables, our lives spared purely because no vehicle came the other way. The hedgerow and my life flashed before me. *I am going to die*, I thought. Then I realized that, no, it would be worse than that: I'd be thrown and left quadriplegic and unable to work. *That is not going to happen*, said my better self, forcing me to sit deep in the saddle and keep my balance. We shuddered into the yard, shaking violently.

I did the thing you're meant to do and got back on, though I hadn't actually got off. We went into the arena and worked on walk, trot, and canter going both ways. We halted nicely. I had control. The pony was calm. I untacked him, paid, went home, and didn't look at a horse again for years. I hadn't known how to handle the situation. There must, I was dimly aware, be things that you could do in that predicament, but I had no shred of a clue what they were, so I wasn't going to put myself, others, or innocent horses in that situation again. This was not relaxation. This was raw terror, and I'd paid good money to end up feeling like that. No more.

So when I started riding Duke, this was front and centre of my mind. I was just waiting for it to happen again – for my equine bluff to be called afresh. It explains, I hope, my fear of tractors and other farm vehicles; why I constantly fear the worst will happen. The combine harvester hadn't caused the problem. Arguably, I had. But it represented what had happened and so became totemic.

With this as my back story, riding out alone is a big achievement, to me at least. And, as I say, Duke and I have been doing more of it. This is the time to go, while the verges are thick with wild flowers, butterflies, and bees. Duke is a particular fan of cow parsley, which has now finished flowering. When it is in flower, he grazes as we ride, which is against the rules of proper riding, but you try stopping three-quarters of a tonne of hungry horse from snacking. July is also a good month for Duke, however, as cow parsley's near-relative, hogweed, is in flower and leaf. This makes for an enjoyable addition to his diet as we head for the woods. Hazel leaves are also popular, and are to be found at head height, so they are easier for Duke to reach without it looking as if he's lunging for the verge. He is not stupid.

I've taken to singing as we ride. It calms me down and regulates my breathing. We see so little traffic generally that there is only a slim chance of being caught out in my eccentricity, though presumably it gives people living along the road a bit of a laugh. I dredge up hymns from my childhood as being rousing and positive, but my favourite is the final movement of *Lux Aeterna* by the contemporary American composer Morten Lauridsen. Yes, I really am singing in Latin whilst riding a horse. The men in white coats will be along shortly. Anyway, the piece of music in question is called *O magnum mysterium*. I first heard it at Winchester Cathedral one Christmas. The cathedral choir is outstanding at the best of times, but singing this it was ethereal. I went physically cold from the emotion of listening to it and wept. This is how it goes, and what I attempt to sing whilst riding Duke along Hampshire's lanes:

> *O magnum mysterium,*
> *et admirabile sacramentum,*
> *ut animalia viderent Dominum natum,*
> *iacentem in praesepio!*
> *Beata Virgo, cuius viscera meruerunt*
> *portare Dominum Christum, Alleluia.*

Snappy, huh? Well, I grant you I won't be winning *Britain's Got Talent* any time soon with that little number, or starting a late-blooming pop career, but my word it's fantastic. If you need convincing, here it is in English:

> *O great mystery and wondrous sacrament,*
> *That the animals should see the newborn Lord, lying in a manger;*
> *Blessed is the Virgin, whose womb was worthy to bear the Lord Christ,*
> *Alleluia.*

Still not sold it to you? What moves me most about this, as you may have guessed, is the idea of the animals being present at Christ's birth. Well, of course they were: he was born in a stable, after all. This would not have been the pretty image of your average Christmas card. Far more likely it was a big area under the inn that was full of all kinds of donkeys and horses belonging to people who'd travelled to Bethlehem for the census. So, as I now understand, the horses would have been trying to establish a herd order, with attendant amounts of kicking, biting, and shoving each other around to get that clear. It wouldn't have been a quiet, relaxing, or even particularly safe place to have a baby. And then there's the poo, which smells fine to me, and the urine, which really doesn't. So it wasn't a clean, sanitary place to bring a baby into the world if you were a teenage girl a long way from home. Yet this is where the pivotal moment of history, of life, happened, if you're a Christian, and horses just like Duke were around to see it happen. Why every horse rider isn't a Christian therefore is a mystery to me, but perhaps no one's told them this. Anyway, it's enough to make me cry.

The great thing about *O magnum mysterium* is that it is very, very slow. However slowly I sing it, I will be too fast. So it's superb for slowing down my breathing and therefore reducing any incipient panic about potential hazards along the route. It's also in Latin, and, as my Latin is sketchy at best, I have to concentrate more on trying to remember the words than I do on thinking about whether a combine harvester is about to block the road and we are going to die. For the record, Duke is not scared of combine harvesters, or tractors, lorries, vans, 4x4s-with-noisy-trailers, horse boxes, cars towing caravans, or even cyclists who appear out of nowhere, silently, and are definitely (from his perspective) neither horses nor vehicles, and therefore potentially frightening. If he sees a farm vehicle, he just plods steadily onwards and walks past it. But, for now, I am still scared of any or all of these, though this will end, and I will wave cheerily at van drivers, smile at farm workers driving impossibly large tractors, and not lose my temper when a caravan cuts us up on a bend in the road, missing us by inches.

This is all still to come, so I am now to be found, on dry mornings, riding up Hensting Lane singing in Latin on a large horse. But, as I've said, my Latin is sketchy, so this means I can't remember all the words. So what I sing actually goes something like this:

O magnum mysterium, something, something, something la,
La la la la la la Dominum natum;
La la la la la la la la la la la laaaaaaa,
La la la la, la la la la, la la la la
portare Dominum Christum la la la.

Not quite as good as the original, I think you'll agree. And this is one of my better days. Sometimes I can remember the first three words (yes, I'm counting "O" as a word) and that's my lot. It doesn't stop me, though, going on and on singing largely wordlessly for half an hour or more. Duke is a patient horse; either that or he doesn't have much Latin either. Though presumably there's not much call for it if you're a horse. No one has yet reported spotting Duke having a furtive read of Ovid in his field.

If my journalistic colleagues found out that I was singing in Latin whilst riding a horse, there would be no end to the ribbing. There is a fiction among some of them that I live on a landed estate, in a modest stately home, and have a butler, gardener, groom, and gamekeeper. We have shoots in the autumn. Indeed, I live almost entirely on game shot on the estate. And, obviously, I ride round my land before heading to work. Wearing tweed.

All this came about, I think, simply because I talk about different things from other people. My water-cooler subjects are horse riding (OK then, Duke), dressage competitions, game, farmers' markets, and, crucially, rural life. Other people, I have noticed, do not talk about these things. This, I firmly believe, makes me rural, not posh. This conclusion is met with howls of derision. The joke started when I was wittering about something and mentioned Phil. "Who's Phil?" someone asked. Quick as a flash, Ed-the-cameraman replied, "The butler." We all laughed. It stuck. The joke grew. We all now refer to it in such a deadpan fashion that one new colleague was sure that I did have a butler and remained so for two years, until I broke it to her gently that, if I could afford a butler *et al.*, I most assuredly wouldn't be working. She remains unconvinced.

Once, while covering a conference in China, I was sitting next to a chap working in international development, whom I knew and liked. We were eating our way through another interminable Chinese banquet as an act of diplomacy, so to pass the time I thought I'd tell him the joke about me being posh. I explained, laughed at how silly it was, and left the floor open for comments.

"Let's do a test," he said. I willingly agreed, knowing myself not to be posh.

"You have a friend who went to finishing school." Er, yes, a Swiss finishing school.

"You have a friend called Jemima." Yes, but we call her "Dormouse" because she is very bad at mornings and is often seen rushing to work late, eating toast.

"You go hunting." No, I prefer dressage. I'm not confident enough to be airborne on a horse.

"You eat game." Seriously, doesn't everyone? It's so cheap.

"You own a pair of green wellies." Of course I do.

"And a Barbour® jacket." I've got two: the really old one is now only presentable enough for cleaning out the chickens and carrying logs into the house.

He laughed at me. "I think they're right," he said. Damn.

Back in the real world (in which I'm not posh, let me re-emphasize), Clare and I travel to Yorkshire to do a fascinating story about a scheme in which every unused piece of ground is taken up and planted with vegetables. It's called Incredible Edible and will soon be nationwide and copied abroad. Right now, it's still little known, but clearly inspiring. We eat peas grown by the side of the road, get hugged by friendly Yorkshire folk, sit in a farmer's garden eating outstanding cheese, and write it all up for *The Mail on Sunday*. It's the kind of story that we both really enjoy. But Clare is not well, having just returned from Bolivia with some kind of bug, and is grey with the concentration required to work when by rights she should be in bed swallowing paracetamol. I feel guilty, as it was my idea to go to Yorkshire and drag her along too.

Once back, my first thought is to head to the stables. This is a remarkable personality change in seven months, but is now such a normal response that I don't notice the change. Kirsten and I meet and decide to work on our drill routine in the outdoor arena. We work on our horses' suppleness and responsiveness for half an hour, with what can best be described as moderate success, and then give it all up as a bad job and head for the really fun bit: fussing about with our horses. We tie them up in the back yard, which is a suntrap even in winter so particularly lovely today, furnish them with apples and water, and get on with the grooming. Duke's feathers and mane have been cut, so he looks very smart and is less itchy. Nonetheless, grooming can take as long as you want it to, so two hours passes like ten minutes in a flurry of different brushes, lotions, sprays, and unguents.

Debbie, another riding buddy, tells me that she used to indulge herself with wonderful moisturizing cream and other beauty products. Now her pony Jack gets all the good products and she buys the cheapest thing possible, probably from a pound shop. Before this year I would have thought her quite mad. Now I totally understand and log the idea of getting my own moisturizer for a pound, mentally totting up what that means I can spend on hoof oil, mane and tail detangler, and equine eye wipes.

Not only is all my spare cash now reserved for meeting Duke's perceived and real needs, my spare time is spent with him too. I run from work to either parent (or both), home to feed George and the hens, and thence to the yard. It is here that – if it is going to be possible – I will relax, and thus ease, if not actually forget, all the stresses of the day. And those stresses continue. They will until my father dies, because I can't make him well by waving a magic wand, even if I had one. And I would give a very great deal to have one. If only, I think, I was Hermione Granger. We see the team at the sweet-smelling care home for one last meeting. Here it is decided that Daddy's stay will be permanent. They will look after him until the end, or until his condition becomes so grave that other levels of care are needed. It's great news, but equally leaves me feeling bereft and empty. I'm extremely thankful to all concerned but desperately sad at the same time.

Phil and our friend Will-the-gardener decide to come and pay my father a visit. I've tried warning them that things have changed, but this is hard to believe until you see it, even if you have medical knowledge, as Phil does. We sit in the dining room of the sweet-smelling care home and are brought an enormous pot of very strong tea and some cake. The cook, I discover, is a dab hand at baking and turns out something delicious every day. For me, it is a complete joy to have company on a visit: not all the conversation falls to me, and we can talk about different things. It's not so great for the lads. They are addressing a man they've known for years who was practical, capable, quirky, and intelligent. Moreover, he knew their names. The person they're talking to now is a shadow of that man and is hazy about who they are, let alone their names or why they are here.

Resolutely positive as always, Phil is full of upbeat plans to keep Daddy busy. He talks about the possibility of Daddy doing some gardening, perhaps in pots, outside, if a member of staff can be found to accompany him. The doors are permanently locked to prevent forgetful people wandering off and getting lost or run over on the main road, so a member of staff is needed just to go out into the garden. There is, Phil says, a shed; that surely could be made into a potting shed. What would Daddy like to grow? He is unsure. How about also feeding the birds, says Phil, knowing my father's dedication to this. Perhaps, says my dad.

Everyone chats away cheerily and my dad looks marginally less confused as time goes on. He still hasn't much of a clue who Phil and Will are, but they are being kind, interesting, and jolly, so it's a diverting way to spend some time. But it is also clearly tiring. After half an hour, he's had it. He stands, slowly but abruptly, shakes their hands, and totters back to his room. It's time to go home. We head for the car and I'm elated because, in my view, it's gone so well. But both Phil and Will – strong, tall, ex-rugby playing types – look shocked and wan, and are on the brink of tears. This is only compounded when I say what a success I think their visit has been. They look horrified.

It's a reminder to me of just how much things have changed and what I now take for granted. To stop the lads weeping openly, we visit some other friends who live nearby. Fran and Richard have two small children (to whom Phil and I are godparents) and vast tracts of land, so we're soon caught up in entertaining the kids and picking vegetables. It's a diversionary tactic, but it works. No one cries, at least not in front of each other.

Because it's official, Daddy's never coming home, my mother and I start to do things that you would normally do only when someone dies: sorting out his stuff. My father's great enthusiasm for and knowledge of the cow parsley family dominated his adult life, his waking hours and thoughts, his holidays, and his garden. Every garden we ever had was full of the plants, grown from seeds garnered from all points across the globe and sent to him by other keen botanists. The greenhouse – with its inner sanctum of a temperature-controlled seed-growing area – was also full of them. Any time you couldn't find my dad, you could bet that's where he would be, tending tiny seedlings with lavish care.

Then there was his study: painted in Farrow & Ball's Book Room Red, carpeted with a large brown Turkish carpet bought from a chap in Turkey who undoubtedly saw my dad (and his credit card) coming, and lined floor-to-ceiling with botanical reference books and file upon file of pressed plants and seeds. Every plant he ever saw, every seed he collected, is here. It is, in all ways, a life's work. As such it will be useful to others who come after him: young fellow botanists, equally desirous to know the difference between one *Ferula* and another. It can't be thrown away. So I call Daddy's old botanical buddies Martin and Sabina Gardiner, now big cheeses at Edinburgh Botanical Gardens. They drive down and fill their car with his life's work and take it back to the Gardens, where it will live on and Daddy's knowledge can be referred to endlessly. Like the situation with the care home, it's wonderful and achingly sad in equal measure.

Mummy then addresses herself to his wardrobe, taking bags of clothes that will never again be needed to her favourite second-hand shop. She asks me questions that I don't want to answer: Would you like your grandfather's wedding ring, which Daddy has kept in a drawer? Would you like Daddy's camera? How about some of his books? I am unprepared for this, as he's still alive and the whole thing has an air of grave-robbing about it, but say "yes" to the important things and take them home and hide them in places where I won't be able to see them every day and feel haunted.

The next day, I wake and find that on no account can I get up, or at least not in any meaningful way. I feed George and the hens and crawl back to bed. Doctors call this "the mind/body connection". Apparently, and perhaps obviously, when you are stressed, anxious or upset, your body tries to tell you something is wrong, in case you've missed it. This can come out in any number of physical symptoms, from diarrhoea to chest pains. But, for me, the symptoms have always been the same: a migraine, which will send me to bed for twenty-four hours, or, as now, extreme tiredness and aches and pains all over. Pals of mine get what they call The Lurgy under similar circumstances: coughing, exhaustion, sickness.

We probably all have our own versions of the body calling a halt on emotional intake. My body is waving the white flag at the ongoing blend of stress, anxiety, grief, tension, and frustration, and is bowing out. Not even a horse can sort this out. So I lie in bed and just let time pass. I am nowhere near singing anything, let alone in Latin. On days like this I know that if it weren't for the need to care for George, the hens, and now Duke, I simply wouldn't get up, ever again. It's not that I'm considering suicide. I'm not. But on my bleakest days I feel that my get-up-and-go has got up and gone, leaving me inanimate, with little interest in life or desire to engage with it.

Time does pass. I do get up again. I have promised to take Mummy away for a couple of nights' stay in a swanky hotel in the New Forest. Since my father became ill she's only been able to have one night away at a time, because of the risks inherent in leaving him alone. Now she can do more than this: a two-night break is a big deal, therefore. We drive down to the New Forest, created in 1079 as a hunting area for William the Conqueror. Its mix of woodland and open ground is kept in check by the ponies, cattle, and pigs of the Commoners, locals who are allowed to let their animals graze there. The swanky hotel wasn't swanky when we first discovered it a few years ago. It was quiet and had deep, old armchairs and extensive grounds abutting woodland, and at night you could see the stars. We loved it.

Now it's been taken over by some very successful hoteliers with a track record of running smart establishments. It's still lovely, but self-consciously smart. Fairly soon we won't be the customer they're after. Reviews will run in national newspapers and it will be a bolt-hole for the smart set from Islington. A potting shed will be turned into a mini spa. You'll be able to borrow wellies, go foraging with a local guide, and eat freshly cooked pizza from a new outdoor oven on the patio. Right now things are in flux, and what we loved about it is still there: the walled kitchen garden, the beehives, ponies in the next field, chickens, the quietness. The peace of the place seeps into both of us and I like to think that some of the furrows in our brows are eased out a little.

We walk in the grounds, read books, and occasionally venture outside the peaceful haven to the rest of the New Forest, which is hardly a bustling metropolis. It is on one of these forays that I separate myself from A Very Large Amount of Money. Somehow, Flick has persuaded me that doing the drill ride is not enough. It is time for Duke and me to do our first dressage test. There's one held about a mile away every month and we can start with the basic walk-and-trot routine. Duke, let it be said, could do much more, and has done in his day. It's my inexperience that requires us to start at the bottom. But it will, Flick assures me, be good experience and a nice day out for Duke. So, much against my better judgment, I have agreed, and a date has been set for early September.

The upside of this is that New Kit is required. I consult both

Flick and the *Horse & Hound* website, somewhat incredulously, and discover that I will need cream jodhpurs, a dark jacket, a shirt and stock or tie, and black knee-length boots. I enter the hallowed portals of Norris's of Beaulieu, the local equestrian store, like a lamb to the slaughter. A kind member of staff listens, works out that I can get away with a child's pair of jods, as I am none too tall, but that the rest needs to be decent quality, and dresses me up. I am wearing the aforementioned cream-coloured child's jods, a pale pink shirt and stock (which looks a bit like a cravat), black knee-length boots, and a dark-navy-nearly-black jacket with gold buttons. My mother is so shocked by the transformation from jeans-wearing journo daughter to smart, presentable person that she has to sit down and be brought a cup of tea to restore her. If you nearly induce a fainting fit in your own mother, quite clearly it's time to buy the outfit. I pretend I can afford it, and do just that. However well Duke and I do on the day, we will look tremendously smart, or at least smarter than we normally do.

August

Through the summer, Annie's arm has been healing slowly. Resolutely positive at all times, she has bitten down on the pain and lied to us about how much it hurts. But it hurts like hell. Worse than the pain has been the fact that for weeks on end she hasn't been able to ride Lady. She comes to the stables sometimes to see the horse, but is so upset by the fact that she can't ride that she often goes away fighting back the tears.

Today is different. Her doctor has said that the bones are healing nicely, so she's managed to persuade him that she's quite safe to ride, just for a few minutes, in the arena. She won't, she promises, do anything rash like go out on a hack. Annie is so charming, so credible, that she could tell you night was day and you'd be tempted to believe her. So she has medical permission to get back on board.

When the big day dawns, she's determined to get Lady ready herself: grooming her and tacking her up as usual. But her left arm is severely weakened and, yes, still causes her pain, so this isn't possible. She is beside herself with frustration. Kirsten and I, who are set to go for a ride in the woods to escape the relentless heat, pretend that nothing is wrong and quietly tack Lady up for her. Kirsten leads Lady out to the mounting block and Annie gets on. She thinks she'll just confine herself to walk and trot, she says. We look at her aghast. She hasn't ridden in weeks and one of her arms is essentially not working.

"Perhaps it might be a plan," I suggest, "just to do walk and halt today. Get your stomach muscles working again. Remember which way to face. Those sorts of things." "Right," she says. "I'll do that." We walk up to the arena with her, and stand in the centre. It is such a huge moment, after months of being away, after the pain, the fear, the what-ifs. Even Annie is scared, her confidence knocked. She sits in the saddle and weeps. We all weep. Then we walk round with her as she and Lady go slowly around the arena, stopping here and there to ensure that Annie has got some brakes. After twenty minutes, Annie is ashen with exhaustion, but beaming broadly. This is what I love about the riding stables: the absolute unquestioning solidarity that people offer each other. Annie and Kirsten have helped, encouraged, chivvied, and supported me. Now it's my turn to help Annie. It reminds me of the community spirit that was abundant in the village chapel in which I grew up: care, support, community, friendliness. It is quite wonderful.

Later, Annie will sit me down in a chilly tack room on a bright winter's day and tell me that I was as much a part of this community spirit as she was. "Before I went back to riding Lady," she will say, "you told me just how frightening it would be, but that I could do it. That really helped me to prepare myself for what would happen."

Apparently – and I'd entirely forgotten this – I had told Annie about the time when I'd recovered from meningitis. After six weeks I'd dragged myself back to the stables, barely able to hold my head up let alone ride, and been poured onto the back of a horse by Flick. It took every ounce of my energy, but it got me out of bed and the house, and thus was worth it. With her arm healed and riding more regularly than the rest of us, Annie still remembered this. "The help wasn't a one-way street," she will tell me.

But now, at the beginning of her rehabilitation, as Annie goes home to have a very well-earned cup of tea, Kirsten and I head for the woods. Kirsten knows that I like to limit the chances of dying on horseback by keeping hacks short. She is determined to get me to go further and to relax and enjoy myself. It is good etiquette, when riding out with others, to ask them which route they would like to take. We discuss it, therefore, and make a plan.

The reality is different. At every junction in the woods she says, "I know we were going to go this way, but it looks cooler this other way. There's more shade. It'd be nice for the horses." So on we go, adding loop after loop to our original half-hour hack, and find ourselves out for a joyous hour and a half. She grins at me as we make our way back to the yard through the last vestiges of dappled shade. "Knew you could do it," she says. I grin sheepishly back, wishing I wasn't such a tense cowardy-custard, but knowing that, eight months in, I still am.

We have one last practice for the drill ride, and I book a final lesson in the manner of a prisoner awaiting execution. But something has clicked in my head. I am actually riding Duke, rather than just sitting on him; asking him politely but firmly to make the bends, semi-circles, serpentines, and loops that I want, and he does them. We are, for once, not arguing about the speed we're going at, whether or not he will work in an outline (which he does), and when and for how long we will halt. After half an hour Flick is uncharacteristically jumping up and down with glee. She praises "perfection" when normally she is hard-pressed to find one small thing we did well. "That made me go cold and all covered with goose bumps," she says with delight. We are, it seems, officially ready. Flick gives me a certificate normally reserved for small children. On it she writes, "Fantastic dressage test. Ten out of ten." I put it on my office wall, where I can see it all the time and be encouraged by it. It is still there today.

The morning of the open day dawns. My friends say that I am a lark, good at mornings. In fact, I am rubbish at them, especially if talking is required within about two hours of getting up. So I arrive at the stables on open day to give Duke a magnificent clean, hoping that I won't have to speak to anyone until the effect of a very early cup of tea has kicked in. No such luck. Everywhere there are small girls with their mothers, washing ponies. It is noisy in a high-pitched, frantic way that can only be achieved by that combination. I try to find a quiet place to groom Duke and fail. Frankly, I'm not entirely sure what I should be doing, except that it's more than a normal brush-down. Flick sees my hesitation and rushes over. She gives me instructions: give Duke a shower; use a gentle shampoo; then towel him dry. When he's dry, we'll hot-cloth him, which will lift any last grot out of his coat. I'm to pay particular attention to his three white socks and nose. They must sparkle. When his socks are clean and dry, chalk is to be added to them to make them pearly white. A product called Show Shine is to be sprayed into his tail. His eyes are to be wiped. And, finally, oil should be applied to his hooves. When I've done all that and tacked him up, I am to go and make myself look smart. And I'm to do all of this in about an hour, which seems utterly impossible.

I start with the hose, washing Duke down, rubbing in a well-known brand of shampoo that's meant to be good for babies, and then hosing him off again, checking all the while that every single bubble has been washed out to avoid irritation and itching. Then it's time to dry him, this enormous horse, with a series of towels that afterwards look as if they'll never recover from the experience. Flick reappears like the shopkeeper in the 1970s children's TV programme *Mr Benn* to hot-cloth him. Someone else pops up and shows me how to apply the chalk. By now, Duke is gleaming in the early-morning sunlight. I spray Show Shine into his tail and every single knot and tangle comes out of it. I wipe his eyes and nose and apply oil to his hooves. Then I tack him up and find that there are about five minutes to go before I too have to be ready. It's a race against time standing in a Portaloo, dragging off mud-spattered clothing and hauling on the New Kit. I run around trying to find someone who knows how to tie a stock, and stand there feeling like a first-year at school having their tie done for them by a sixth-former. But at the end of it, I look as smart as I ever have, except possibly when wearing a ball gown, and we are ready to go.

The public (for which read friends and family of everyone who rides at the stables, plus a few people who have read about it in the local paper) have started to arrive. They are directed up to a makeshift car park behind the arena, which is normally a field for some of the horses. Members of a local Army corps are kindly doing the honours, and so everything is running smoothly. The day-to-day car park has been converted into Fun Central. There is a barbecue going already, a cake stall, plenty of stalls selling things you don't need, a tempting one that's touting supplements for horses, a raffle, bunting, and lots of very loud music. All the horses have been given a calmer to stop them spooking at such scary objects and sounds. Except Duke. I am appalled. What will happen to us? Flick looks at me pityingly. "He'll be fine," she says. "Honestly, he doesn't need it."

"Then give it to me instead," I beg her, looking hopefully at the syringe of apple-flavoured calmer. She laughs and wanders off to get proceedings under way.

The rest of the morning is a bit of a blur. I have no recollection of the staff drill ride. I may, at some point, have had a cup of tea, though clearly not whilst riding. Time drags and rushes simultaneously. Then it's time to go and do our stuff. Can I remember the moves that I've practised, walking round the kitchen like a mad woman? Can I take the lead, stay level with another horse and rider, keep calm, and come out at the end with my dignity intact, or will I make a complete howling idiot of myself and let Duke down? It appears that I can keep calm, ride well, and remember the moves after all. However, for me the next five minutes are full of sweat, fear, and concentration. For Duke they are no bother at all. He does as he's bidden, not making any errors, and comes calmly to a halt at the end without one spook at the loudspeakers, bunting, dogs, children, and general unfamiliarity of it all.

I am euphoric. We did it! People pat Duke fondly and congratulate him and smile at me vaguely as if I merit some recognition, but not much. I pat Duke too, find carrots for him, and wish profoundly that I could get back on and do it all again. Where did that desire come from?

Then, between events, Duke is taken away to give pony rides (some pony), and I am bereft. All I want to do is sit in a stable and congratulate the horse that I now see as mine (though he isn't) on a solidly good performance, drink tea, and give him a post-exercise groom. Later, several hours later, this happens. I sit on my tack box in the shade while Duke chews his hay, and find myself thinking, *One day I'd like to own Duke.* This feeling has crept up on me slowly, quietly, thoroughly unexpectedly. I am not, after all, a horsey person. But now I am convinced that, above all things, I want to spend my days caring for this wonderful, solid, soulful horse. What's stranger is that it doesn't feel like a surprise. It is the most natural thing in the world, like saying that you want to marry the person you've fallen in love with, or take a job at your favourite newspaper. But if you'd told me in January that by August I'd want to buy this horse, I would have dismissed the notion as folly.

The afterglow of our extremely minor triumph goes some way to providing emotional ballast for the rest of life. But, like the return to work after a holiday, it can't last long. The weather is still good, so I decide to bring Daddy to my house to have a cup of tea in the back garden. I can't take him to his garden or we'll never get him back to the care home. But he's helped me plant and care for my garden over the years, so it'll do as second best. As I look around the garden, many memories arise of working on it with my dad. It was very pleasant when I moved in, but it wasn't mine. Slowly, I allowed my stamp to be put on it, cutting down things that I didn't like and planting things that I did. In the end I had a wholesale change, as Fran and Phil spent a couple of weekends turning it into an English cottage garden, complete with espaliered apple trees, borders full of alliums, and plenty of my favourites, clematis and roses. My dad always helped: dug, advised, and planted. One Boxing Day, very early on, we planted canes of red- and blackcurrants as well as gooseberries, while the snow fell around us and our hands seized up with the cold.

Having grown up near beech woods, I wanted to be reminded of them, and loved nothing more than beech trees. My garden was obviously far too small for a towering beech, but not for beech hedges. My father liberated about twenty seedlings from the woods at the end of our old road and helped me plant them into a hedge that lined two sides of the far end of the garden. At first they were tiny little scraps. Now they were ten feet high and home to robins and blackbirds that raise their chicks there. He'd helped affix an extremely Heath Robinson garden light and put up water butts.

He knew that garden as well as I did. I felt sure that a cup of tea on the patio would be just the thing to cheer him up. Once again, I hadn't reckoned with the dementia. We drive gently back to my house, with me treating him like a cross between a tray of eggs and the Crown Jewels: something to take care of whilst driving. We arrive home and he looks puzzled, but follows me in. I make tea and we sit outside, in the garden that he's helped tend for years. "What do you think of the garden?" I say.

"It looks nice," he replies. "Where are we?" Oh, dear God. I explain that we're at my house. I show him things he planted. He looks at them mystified, as if he's never seen them before. But then if the last thing he can confidently remember is living by the village common aged four, my garden is going to make no sense at all. And it doesn't.

Accordingly, therefore, the outing isn't what you'd call a roaring success. I'd hoped for a happy hour in the sunshine drinking tea, with Daddy at least in familiar surroundings. Instead, he is somewhere strange and clearly feels anxious. I drive him back to the care home, thinking this will put things to rights. It doesn't, because he can't remember that he lives there either. On days like this I resort to shopping just to cheer myself up. My favourite comfort-buy is a bunch of flowers from a family-run garage on the edge of the city. They have lovely blooms at very affordable prices and the people are friendly. I stop there a lot at the moment. I do so today.

Since he's been in care, Daddy's found it harder and harder to remember where he lives, which must be terrifying – like feeling permanently lost and not knowing how to get home, or indeed where home is in the first place. He asks repeatedly if the house is OK, who's looking after it, how the garden is, is it all going to rack and ruin? No, I say, it's all fine. I'm looking after it; so is Fran, so is Phil. I take him pictures of the house that he's lived in for the last fifteen years, just to prove that it hasn't all fallen down in his absence, and he doesn't recognize it. Neither does he remember the years that he lived in Fareham with the massive garden and the hand-dug well. Sadly, now he can't even remember our gorgeous family home in the village. But as he remembers the village itself, I stop trying to pretend that the last forty years existed and plump for the brick-and-flint house by the common in which he was born, which will outlast us all. That is officially home.

There are days when I can cope with this. But, frankly, mostly

I can't. My father's memory has poured, like sand, out of his ears, and I am talking to someone who has no memory of my life, or of much of his own. It's enough to keep you awake at night, staring at the ceiling, which it does. I've had two good nights' sleep in the last six months. If you've never had insomnia, it can be hard to imagine just how it grinds you down. But, apparently, every year a third of us will suffer from it, so I am clearly not alone. If you get to sleep at 4 a.m., it is hard to drag yourself out of bed when the alarm goes off two hours later. If you do sleep, but are plagued with nightmares and wake repeatedly, this can leave you exhausted too. Or there's the old favourite: tossing and turning all night, waking feeling that you haven't slept a wink. I do the lot, and more besides: the long, wakeful hours between 3 a.m. and 6 a.m. are the worst, haunted by dreadful visions of the future. If something's going to look bad, it will do so at 4 a.m.

The excellent NHS website has tips on what to do if you suffer from insomnia. Keep regular hours, it says. Make sure that you go to bed at roughly the same time every night. I do this. Create a restful sleeping environment and make sure your bed is comfortable. My bed is absurdly comfortable and the room is just as I would want it to be: light, airy, and cool. Exercise regularly, says the website. Have I mentioned Duke? Drink less caffeine. Don't be ridiculous, I say. Everyone has to have a vice. Mine are tea and cheese. A person has to die of something. Don't overindulge, the website says; not too much eating and drinking late at night. Chance would be a fine thing, I mutter, but may I refer you to my previous answer about tea and cheese? I'm not drinking neat gin and eating boxes of chocolates. How bad can it be? Don't smoke, says the website. Never have. Never will. Really, why would I?

Then come the last three killer tips: try to relax before bedtime; write away your worries; and don't worry in bed. These three seem to me to have been written by someone very well-intentioned who's never had a care in their life, and certainly hasn't got a parent with dementia and another one recovering from a stroke. The minute I lie down my brain starts whirring its way through a list of what is happening, might happen, could happen, a whole panoply of worst-case scenarios, and what is real: that I can't change any of this and it will only get worse. This, dear NHS, is quite enough to keep the most sanguine person awake all night, no matter how comfortable their bed or how little tea they drink.

Did you know, says the website, which I'm starting to view as my personal enemy, that lack of sleep can have profound consequences for your physical health? Lack of sleep, it says, puts you at risk of serious medical conditions, including obesity, heart disease, and diabetes. And, it says, getting out its trump card and slapping it down on the table, it shortens your life expectancy.

Oh, that really is great, I grumble at the screen. Not only am I in a permanently bad mood (unless I've seen Duke), my brain isn't functioning properly and I ache all over, but now you tell me that this not-sleeping lark is also taking years off my life? Believe me, I want to sleep. I *long* to sleep. I would probably at this stage give you a few years off my life, if it meant I could sleep and wake up refreshed again, rather than haggard. So it is that Clare and I hop on a series of planes up to Orkney on a reporting assignment, and I find myself hoping that, if nothing else, I will sleep.

Possibly, without the invention of the mobile phone, I would have done. But as it is, Daddy continues to ring from the care home and I check every night that my mother is still alive. It's like a little cloud of gloom that hovers over me and won't disperse despite the absolutely stunning surroundings we find ourselves in. Orkney is in fact an archipelago of seventy islands off the north of Britain, twenty of which are inhabited. We are on the largest, known as Mainland, which tells you all you need to know about focus, size, and the relevance of the rest of the UK. We hire a car, in a howling gale that presumably passes for a light summer breeze up here, and drive about Mainland interviewing farmers, local celebrities, vicars: everyone we can think of.

And when it's all done, miraculously we have a bit of spare time. Believe me, this never happens. Our normal trips involve twelve- to eighteen-hour days, worked back to back, with just about enough time to lie down and sleep (or not) before you start all over again. Not that we're complaining; we love it. But it just so happens that we find ourselves one afternoon with the stories for that day in the bag and an hour to kill at one of the world's finest archaeological sites, Skara Brae.

But it's closed. That howling gale is howling so much that it's unsafe to walk even the short distance from the visitor centre to the site. I can well believe it. You wouldn't need to be Mary Poppins with an umbrella to take off in this weather. Clare is devastated. She is a geographer even more than she is a photographer (and having reported from all points round the world, she's certainly that), and she loves all things ancient. So Skara Brae was on her bucket list.

The next morning the howling gale has blown itself out and we head back to Skara Brae, which is now open. This is a Neolithic settlement: a village that dates back some 5,000 years, but gives the impression that everyone just walked out a few hours ago. Small dwellings were constructed under the earth for insulation and safety. One runs on to the next and you get a feel for community life, people living cheek by jowl with each other, carrying out day-to-day tasks. It may be ancient, but it's recognizable. There are areas for sleeping and sitting, stone sideboards and lintels, mantelpieces and fireplaces. You know just at a glance where everything belongs, where the different events of the day take place.

Anything ancient gives one a sense of perspective. The city walls around Winchester have that effect on me. I look at them and think of all the people who have come and gone, flourished, prospered, and died while the walls have been there. They represent permanence in our constantly changing, fluctuating, uncertain world. They always make me feel better. Skara Brae has the same effect.

I get seven hours' sleep… and wake to discover that all round Britain there are riots. It's like watching news reports from foreign climes. It makes absolutely no sense up here, where we are draped in history, eating cheese made by local farmers, and, yes, honestly, interviewing people. Everyone's mystified. We're mystified. Will the riots come to Mainland? It's about as likely as Duke and me winning the Grand National. I get another seven hours' sleep.

While I've been having a jolly time reporting in Orkney, Duke has been festooned with small-children-who-don't-normally-ride during the summer holidays. He is an equable creature, slow to anger and long on patience, but he is resoundingly pissed off. He's worked hard and not much of it has been any fun at all. He explains this to me by doing the exact opposite of everything I ask, as we ride for the first time on my return. If I ask for halt, he'll set his mouth against me and walk on, or lunge for the grass, or both. If I ask for trot, he will walk. If I ask for walk, he will trot. And if I ask for an outline, he gets completely enraged and we argue about who's going to win. My arms turn to water and he wins. I can't blame him. If I'd worked as hard as he has done and the consolation prize was me, I'd be fed up too.

It poses a question: how do you communicate effectively with a horse? Over the years, in various places, I've seen varyingly successful kinds of communication. Some of it has been quiet and trustworthy. But a lot of it has been akin to slamming the lid of the photocopier down when you're cross about something at home, or smashing the crockery when you're upset. Much of it has been ignorant, some of it cruel, still more misguided. However, as a newcomer to horses, I don't know what's right. Gut instinct tells me what's wrong: shouting, pushing, barging, losing your temper. These don't work with people, so why would they work with horses? Gut instinct also tells me that horses are never "rude", "stupid", "silly", or "bad": terms that I hear used all the time. How can a horse be bad, I wonder? It's just reacting to what's happening around it. The sum of all this is that I'm looking for a language with which to communicate with horses, as I'm sure that some of the ones I have seen used aren't quite working. Imagine talking in English to someone who is French, and their not understanding. Then imagine your response being to shout the same thing again. It's not going to work, is it? And it makes you look like an idiot.

So I'm off to learn the equine equivalent of French. And there's only one place to learn: an organization based at the home of the horse, Lambourn in Berkshire. Monty Roberts, thought by many to be the original inspiration behind the novel and film *The Horse Whisperer*, has been an advisor to the Royal Stables for twenty-five years. He trains Her Majesty's young horses, spends time with any of her horses that face problems, and also assists with Prince Philip's horses.

More than this, he's come up with a way of communicating with horses that uses the same body language they use in a herd, but no speech and no touch. He calls this "join-up", where through making a horse go away from him, he brings out the herd instinct, making it want to come to him. When it does, it will follow him anywhere, and the leader–follower roles are set. This sounds like exactly what I need: a system of communicating with

Duke that is based on the equine language he speaks, makes me act like a leader, and gives Duke the chance simply to be a horse, not the responsible member of the partnership. And, frankly, if it's good enough for the Queen, who is an amazing horsewoman, then it's most certainly good enough for me.

I've signed up for a two-day course run by Monty Roberts' British protégée, Kelly Marks. It's called "Perfect Manners". My guess is that this is about my manners being made perfect, not the horse's. The first thing we learn is how to lead each other, which reveals all our weaknesses and faults. Then we practise "join-up" on a person just so that we can remember all the moves. Then they bring the horses in. Everyone does terribly well. Then it is my turn. I get stage fright standing in the large indoor arena surrounded by fellow horse enthusiasts. Everything I've learned all day goes out of the window. I rush. I lack energy and intention, says Kelly. And, frankly, you could say that I lack energy and intention every day of the week, not just when I get on a horse. (There's a clue there, methinks.) But still, Reuben the horse does come to me and I feel like weeping with delight. Even if you speak French badly, it's better than speaking no French at all. My French, as it were, may be a bit rubbish at the moment, but it'll get better.

The next day, we do it all again. This time, they give me a less straightforward horse. He's enormous! I'm terrified. But I remember what I've been taught, rush slightly less, act with a bit more energy and intention than on day one, and by some kind of equine miracle, the horse comes to me. This time I do weep. Monty Roberts says that "good trainers can hear horses talking to them; great trainers can hear them whisper". I want to hear every word that Duke says and now I feel as if I have a chance. But how do I translate this wonderful two-day experience away from home onto Duke back at the stables? We don't have the facilities to do join-up and I'd feel daunted doing it by myself. Mercifully, help is at hand in the shape of the ever-smiling Sarah Weston, a local specialist in what is known as Intelligent Horsemanship. One inclement wet day, she joins Duke and me at the yard. I've booked the outdoor arena, which is looking more like a pond because it's rained so much, in order that we can put some of Kelly Marks' and Monty Roberts' teaching into practice.

You need a round pen to do join-up. We don't have one. So the next best thing is groundwork exercise. First, this involves Sarah teaching me how to move Duke's feet just by looking at them. When I can do this, she gets me to move him forward and back, side to side. If this sounds like magic, all I can suggest is that you watch two horses out in a field. This is what they do to each other. Duke does this. He is unquestionably head of the herd. This means that he gets first dibs of the best hay when it's brought to the field. He lumbers gently towards it. In his way is a small pony called Jack, one of his field mates. Duke looks at Jack's shoulder, then at his feet, and Jack moves – moves right away from the hay, which he'd really like to eat, because Duke has silently, quietly told him to clutter off.

We do this and it works. Duke goes backwards, forwards. Stands still. I am head of the herd. He is Jack. He is doing as he's asked. As if that wasn't good enough, Sarah then sets up a dog-leg slalom course, using jump poles to mark the edges. First, I'm to walk Duke through it forwards, stepping backwards myself like a TV cameraman. "The trick," she says, "is to ensure that you take it so slowly that his feet don't touch the poles. If they do, you have to start again." So we do this step by slow step, with me looking at his feet, using my shoulders and body to guide him, but not touching him, not even speaking, let alone raising my voice. I am calm. He is calm. We get round the course without a foot touching the poles – either mine or his. I am thrilled. "Right," says Sarah, "now do it all in reverse." "You *are* kidding," I say. "Do the whole thing backing him up round corners that he can't see?" "Yes," she says. "The same rules apply. Away you go." And we do, cautiously, gently, back round the dog-leg course.

A whole Blackpool illuminations of lights go on in my head. This is equine French. I have spoken. Duke has understood and obliged. And it's so useful. Now I'll know how to reverse him into a stable, or out of one; how to lead him past the everyday slalom of yard life: wheelbarrows, pitchforks, small children. I might even be able to take him up to the field without him lunging for grass. We practise walking up and down the track past what is essentially a Chinese takeaway for Duke, and it's better than normal. It's not lunge-free, but I can rectify the problems more quickly. Duke is listening. I am not losing my temper out of frustration – with myself that I don't know what to do, more than with him. Sarah smiles, as if she has imparted great wisdom to a new student, which she has. "Duke," she says, "is one of the sweetest, most benevolent and polite horses I have ever met. He was", she says, "so attentive and sensitive and all the other superlatives you can think of."

Hoorah. Hoorah. I'm not wrong. Like Gene Kelly, I want to sing and dance in the rain. I am not riding some stupid old plod of a horse, as, just ever so occasionally, some people hint that I might be. I am officially riding "one of the sweetest, most benevolent and polite horses" that a highly experienced and well-reputed trainer has ever met. Duke is confirmed in being fabulous. Get the bunting out. More than this, I am finally, finally starting to learn how to talk to him. We stand in the rain in the outdoor arena and look at one another. He's worked hard all morning, so should be tired, but above all things he seems relieved. "Thank goodness," he appears to be saying. "You've finally understood what I've been trying to say to you all these months."

"I'm sorry I've been so slow, Duke," I say.

He blinks slowly and nods.

Flick wanders over. "Did Duke get it?" she asks.

"Duke got it all perfectly," I say. "He knew it all along. It was me that had to learn, and after today, yes, I think I'm getting there."

September

Why do people read horoscopes? I don't, you see, and the idea has always mystified me. First, there must be millions of us born on the same day, so how can a couple of lines in a newspaper accurately cover what's going to happen to us all? Second, what have today's events got to do with stars in the sky? And, third, this really is just a couple of lines of newspaper text. It's written to length and to deadline. Is anyone seriously suggesting that this is accurate or life-predicting?

We all know it's tosh, don't we? But, interestingly, according to Dr Margaret Hamilton, a psychologist from the University of Wisconsin, 70 per cent of newspaper horoscopes are positive. This is a higher rate than the rest of the average newspaper's content, in all probability, so people read horoscopes for light relief, she says. *Psychologies* magazine adds, "Horoscopes offer escape from daily anxieties – grown-up fairy tales many of us consume without questioning." The art with horoscopes is to be vague but positive, so we can all identify with them. So, for instance, my horoscope for this month could read, "Things have been a little tricky for you in the past, but there are opportunities for improvement." But had I seen an accurate horoscope (if that's not an oxymoron) for this month, I wouldn't have got out of bed, let alone got on an aeroplane. This was to be the month in which my life would change for ever – when I thought it already had.

"It's September," says Clare as we drive to Heathrow Airport. "It must be Ethiopia. Again."

We're heading back to Ethiopia for the second time in the year. We get our jabs, passports, and tickets, and head for the airport. Everything seems normal, but it's a trip that will be very costly for my health and my career. Right now, I don't know this. I'm just on the M3 heading back to Heathrow and Ethiopia. What could possibly go wrong?

Quite a lot, as it turns out. Our earlier trip to Ethiopia had been a success: we'd got the stories we needed, travelled safely, and stayed well, and our fixer had understood what we needed, which is invariably the key to a satisfactory assignment. We'd loved the country and the people. None of this is the case the second time around.

Our first problem, on returning, is that it's the wet season. The large amount of rain, and sometimes flash floods, can make driving in an underdeveloped country very difficult. You try getting to remote villages if you haven't got a 4x4 and the roads have been washed away. It's virtually impossible, hugely time-consuming, and bad for your health. You spend all your time making unnecessarily hard journeys when you should be sitting around listening to people's stories.

We end up walking through mud for an hour or so after a six-hour drive to get to one village. Then, having chatted to people and got some pictures, we do the whole thing in reverse. It's madness. And every day is a variant on this. One night we stay in a lodge that lies a two-hour drive up a totally perilous road, along which we quite genuinely fear that we will die. That's fearless Clare thinking we're going to die, not just me, so it must be bad. When we get there the food is cold and inedible, the beds cold and damp. Clare rips down the shower curtain and wraps herself in it in a bid to sleep and stay dry simultaneously. And why are we here? Because our fixer thinks we'll like it. How wrong he is.

The second problem is that our fixer is quite young. As we are doing church-based stories, this means that he is continuously dealing with older church leaders, who pull rank on him. He is unable or unwilling to negotiate with them. So we have a schedule that reads, "Interview people in village A about story B", and what we get is a whole load of sitting about waiting for church leaders, then waiting for more of them, a bit of eating, and then a whole entourage of unnecessary people dragging along to some remote village and getting in our way while we try to interview the locals.

This happens every day for a week. It is like pushing a boulder up a hill, repeatedly, hour after hour, day after day. We are both strung out with the dual perils of trying to move our fixer beyond his deference to clerics and into helping us with our stories, and getting enough material to hit our deadlines. This is quite enough, but one day, just for a bit of variety, we have a car crash. If you travel abroad frequently, a car accident is the thing you fear most. There are a lot of truly crazy drivers out there.

Beijing is memorable, and not in a good way. Seeing cars drive onto a motorway and along it on the wrong side, against oncoming vehicles, in order to avoid a crash on the correct side, will live long in the memory, particularly as some of them were police cars. Mumbai, however, was worse. I spent a great deal of time with my eyes shut expecting a crash as we were driven round there. But the blow never came. So it was actually a bit of a surprise when a lorry drove into our side in Ethiopia.

We'd been given a vehicle without seatbelts, and were driving back to the hotel after another reasonably fruitless day of interviewing. Out of the corner of my eye I could see an enormous aid lorry, taking grain to a refugee camp. It was monstrous, far bigger than our little vehicle. And it was going fast, heading straight for our flank. There was a moment when everything in my head slowed right down. *That truck's not stopping,* I thought. *It really is going to hit us. I can't believe it.* And then BANG! It did hit us. We all went flying, thanks to the absence of seatbelts.

After we'd ascertained that no one had broken any bones, we all got out of the vehicle to enquire of the lorry driver what he meant by it. He had, he said, been driving for forty hours non-stop to deliver the grain to refugees. He simply couldn't go any further. He had to stop and rest.

"Did it not occur to you", we asked, "just to pull over by the side of the road and sleep?"

"That's the problem," he said, naming a very large aid agency for whom he worked. "They won't let me. They tell me I just have to get there. The only way I'm allowed to stop is if I crash, so I crashed."

"Thanks very much," we said. "We don't wholly appreciate being caught in your need-for-sleep driving manoeuvres."

Truthfully, I feel sorry for the man. If his story is true – and there's no reason to disbelieve him – then he's in a terrible fix.

Also in a bit of a fix is our vehicle, which has come off decidedly second best. A crowd of men has appeared out of nowhere. Everyone is shouting. There is quite a bit of argy bargy, with people pushing and pulling each other around comically, though no one is badly hurt. Then there's considerable yelling about the vehicle and about the two white women. Get them out of here, seems to be the general consensus, whichever side of the scuffle you are on. Another vehicle appears and we are borne off back to the hotel while the row continues in the middle of the road.

You'd think you'd be safe in a hotel, wouldn't you? Though, having said that, I've done the mandatory Foreign Travel Security course, which gives the lie to all that. I've learned to memorize quick routes out of hotels in case of fire, attack, or worse; to put a wooden wedge under my door at night to keep it jammed shut against rapists and kidnappers; to have a medical kit about my person at all times, and, having reported in the former Soviet Union, to believe unquestioningly that walls have ears.

And it's in the hotel that I think it happens. I get bitten by a mosquito: another hazard of the wet season, when they swarm over still and stagnant water. There is plenty of that outside the hotel, so there are clouds of mosquitoes too. Now, I'm being sensible: wearing light-coloured clothing, covering up my arms and legs, and spraying myself with mosquito repellent. But the hotel has the air of a place thrown up optimistically in five minutes flat, and there are gaps between the windows and their casements. It's through one of these that, I suspect, the little blighter gets in.

The mosquito may be small, but it is officially the deadliest creature in the world. Never mind being eaten by a lion, rushed at by a rhino, or bitten by a snake; it's the mosquito that will get you. There are some 3,500 varieties of mosquito, many of which live off the blood of humans. As they pass from person to person, they can carry some pretty nasty diseases, including malaria and yellow fever. I'm taking the tablets for malaria and have had the yellow fever jab. So I feel that I'm one step ahead of the mozzies. But I haven't reckoned with a whole string of other serious illnesses that they carry, including West Nile virus, dengue fever, filariasis, and other arboviruses.

I get bitten. So does Clare. This always happens. A few days later, I notice that my body is covered in tiny red dots. It doesn't look like a rash. Perhaps it's some kind of sand fly bite, I think, illogically, as there is no sand. Anyway, it doesn't itch, so I am unperturbed. On our last day, we are standing in a dark, small church when I start to feel decidedly odd. Every bone in my body hurts. I don't have the energy to stand up. And I am very, very cold.

"Is it cold in here, Clare?" I hiss, trying not to interrupt the proceedings.

"No," she says, looking at me askance; "it's boiling hot."

Oh darn, says my worse self; something is not right here. But as I am prone to melodrama and hypochondria, I shake off the notion that finally I've got some dreadful tropical disease, and assume that I'm just exhausted. It's been a gruelling week, after all. That evening we take our hosts out for dinner to thank them for facilitating us, which we do with a straight face and a light heart, because we know that tomorrow we'll be on our way home. That night I start to feel a bit groggy and spend a bit more time in the bathroom than I'd like. Something I ate, I tell myself; nothing to worry about.

The next morning it transpires that actually, yes, it is something to worry about. We are taking a night flight home, so I spend the day quietly between the bedroom and the bathroom. Still it doesn't occur to me that this is anything other than Traveller's Tummy. The airport at Addis Ababa is not for the faint-hearted, let alone the faint. A member of staff spots that I'm looking a tad peaky and upgrades us to business class for the overnight flight to Frankfurt, where we will change planes and head back to Heathrow. We are never normally upgraded, so this is a whole lot of fun no matter how wretched I feel. We play with the buttons on the seats like a couple of children and even manage to get four hours' sleep.

So when we arrive at Frankfurt Airport at Horrid O'Clock, I should be marginally refreshed. But I'm not. I'm starting to feel decidedly worse. We get to our gate and I go to the toilet repeatedly, holding on to the walls for support, dragging my feet, all energy gone. "We're nearly there," says Clare. "All you have to do is get onto this plane." So I summon one last burst of energy and drag myself onto the plane, concentrating on putting one foot in front of the other as a deliberate act of will. We get as far as the purser and present our tickets. But no further. "You're not looking very well, madam," he says.

"I'm fine," I say. "I just want to go home." And I promptly faint.

The next few hours are hazy. The purser is adamant that I am not well enough to fly. I cry, beg, and beseech him to let me get on this flight and go home to my bed, where, I absolutely promise, I will be fine. But he's having none of it. "We are not medically trained, madam," he says. "We can't look after you if you get worse."

"I'm not going to get worse," I say, unrealistically. "I'll just sit quietly and soon we'll be home."

Instead, paramedics are called. Then there is a comedy about whether I have travel health insurance that will cover me. I do. Incoherently, I call the company in the UK and check whether it's OK for me to get taken to an airport hospital in Germany, because I appear to have collapsed. Yes, they say, that's fine. Just get a reference number. Nothing simpler when you are sick. But anyhow, I do it and the next thing I know I'm in a hospital at the airport.

This is where things start to go from bad to worse. I explain where I've been. The kindly German doctor takes the view that the most likely thing is some kind of Traveller's Tummy. It is. But how wrong could he be? I haven't got "the most obvious thing". He pumps me full of two litres of saline, as I am badly dehydrated and have skin that looks like an old tortoise. For the next five hours I lapse in and out of consciousness as quiet, efficient nurses come in to change the saline bags. When I wake, I'm whisked off to a waiting plane with Clare, our baggage having been rescued and redirected. It's impressive and a relief. I think it's all over, as they say in footballing parlance. But it isn't.

I don't remember the flight home. But I do remember the cab ride back with Clare afterwards. Again I'm lapsing in and out of consciousness, but trying to pretend that I'm sleeping in order not to worry her. But she is worried.

"Your eyes are red and your head's all swollen," she says.

"Seriously, Clare," I say, "I'm fine. It's just a bug of some sort; nothing to worry about."

And we both go very quiet, because we both know that it *is* something to worry about. Over the next few days I appear to stage a recovery. I'm weak and achingly, achingly exhausted. I can't write. But I get up and potter about and watch old episodes of *Spooks*, my habit when below par. A week later I attempt to leave the house and walk down the hill. It feels like a marathon. And I've lost weight; I'm down to 7 stone 7. I feel as if the stuffing has been knocked out of me.

I am quite sure that I cannot possibly do the dressage competition that Duke and I are entered in a few days later. I've barely got beyond the sofa. How can I drive to the yard, get Duke ready for a competition, ride to that competition, take part, ride back, and clean him up again? I explain this to Flick. But she is used to me ducking out of things through fear and won't have any of it. I haven't even seen Duke for a fortnight, but we are set to compete for the first time.

A nearby livery yard plays host to monthly dressage competitions throughout the summer. There's plenty of scope for advanced riders, who come from far and wide in a huge variety of horse lorries. But for Duke and me there is a simple walk-trot test. It will take about five minutes and we are to perform a series of moves, circles, half-circles, serpentines, bends, and changes of rein going both ways around the outdoor school. The point of this is to show that Duke is as supple one way as he is the other, which he isn't, and that I am a sufficiently competent rider to get him to do his moves at fixed points, which I doubt that I am.

But with Flick metaphorically barring the door behind me, there is no way back, however ill I feel. I am to compete.

So, one Saturday morning when all sensible people are still fast asleep, I am up at 5.30 a.m. and arrive at the yard at 6.45. Flick is there, ever positive and resilient. We get Duke ready, polishing him until he shines. I have separated myself from a three-figure sum for my own saddle and bridle, so we look as smart as we are ever going to. Flick has docked Duke's somewhat raggedy mane and trimmed his tail and the feathers on his legs. I don the New Kit and take a deep breath. I'm not sure which I'm more nervous about: the ride to and from the competition or the competition itself. We've practised both, so there is nothing to worry about, but I like to worry. It gives me something to do.

The reason I'm worried about the route is that it involves two main roads, not just friendly, quiet little Hensting Lane where we know everyone by sight and even the tractor drivers stop and allow us to go past, turning off their engines to avoid spooking the horses. We will be faced with Proper Traffic. What will happen then?

We turn left out of the yard and along Hensting Lane, passing all the big houses that dot either side of the road, and get closer and closer to the main road that runs from Winchester to Bishop's Waltham and Wickham. You'd hardly call this a motorway, but cars can go at 60 mph and this poses a risk to horse and rider. Equally, drivers on the main roads aren't used to seeing horses there, so they are not quite as prepared and perhaps not quite as patient as the drivers along Hensting Lane. Above and beyond all this, there are traffic lights. Traffic lights are, I grant you, not as fearsome as a roundabout. But this is the first time I have negotiated them and I am shaking with fear at the prospect.

Flick decides to come with me, saddles up her mount, and rides as if she were heading out for a picnic. We get to the first of the two main roads and I am white with fear. "All right?" she says, glancing back over her shoulder.

"Absolutely fine," I lie. We trot down to the traffic lights in a bid to get it over more quickly. Lorries pass us: huge, enormous, pantechnicon lorries. I think we might die. Duke doesn't turn a hair and carries on trotting, ears pricked, conscious that we are out Doing Something Different, which in itself has to be fun. Flick beams. "He's such a good horse," she says. "Give him a pat." I duly do, simply for the distraction it will give me for a few seconds from the terror that is going along a main road in the countryside. We get to the lights and wait. Cars give us a wide berth and when the lights finally go green we are on our way, trotting along the second, faster, main road.

If you really want to spook a horse, ride along there. It looks like the heart of rural England, with farms to right and left, a clutch of houses set back from the road, two pubs, and the occasional small business venture. There is plenty of woodland and it is just a stone's throw from Marwell Zoo. That's what it's like in a car. On the back of a horse, it's another matter. There are signs that flap, others that spin. Someone has put long, flapping signage flags outside their business. These are the equivalent of ghosts to a horse and I fully expect Duke (who has not seen them before) to leap sideways into the traffic at the sight of them. He does not. He is not spooked by the fast cars (and here people aren't slowing down, but whizzing past us at 60 mph), the lorries, the farm vehicles, the unfamiliar scenery, the bins ready for collection, or any other nameless horror that marks our route. It is, therefore, with a sense of triumph that we turn right, through the traffic, and into the livery yard where the competition is to be held.

I feel as if I've done a day's work already, but it is still only 8.45 a.m. Normally I'd barely be up and about at this time on a Saturday. This horse business has taken a serious hold of my brain and time, as well as my finances. I'm competing just after 9 a.m. Flick has managed my expectations by saying that anything over 30 per cent will be fine first time out. She is, I know, saying this because she expects me to have a major wobble and go to pieces, not because 30 per cent would be fine.

I am determined to do all her teaching and patience justice and do better than that. I forget that I feel absolutely terrible and we head for the practice ring. Here, everyone who is competing early is practising their routine, going through sections that they find difficult, in and out of the different paces. There is a rule that you must pass each other left-to-left, so, as well as trying to remember what we're doing in an unfamiliar setting, I have to negotiate other horses and riders. Duke finds the whole thing too much and is spooked by unseen ghouls in the hedgerow. But somehow we hold it together and, very quickly, a friendly young woman with a clipboard comes to the gate and calls our names.

We walk towards the competition arena with me feeling like a member of the French royal family on the way to the guillotine, and Duke pricking his ears with a mix of excitement and nervousness, mostly the former. He appears to have grown about six inches and is quivering with excitement. Flick has handed her horse Joe to someone and walks by our side. "Smile," she says. "You can do this."

And then we're off. The drill is that you trot into the arena and, when a whistle blows, ride to the judges' box, salute, and present yourself and your horse. Then you are allowed to perform your competition routine. We are trotting nicely along the long side of the outdoor school when Duke spots the judges' box, and takes an instant dislike to it. He turns himself round and heads for home: this from a horse who seldom spooks at anything. My nerves must be transmitting themselves to him. We are not doing that, says my better self, and I turn him round, get him to the judges' box, salute, apologize that things have gone wrong before we've even started, present us both, and then away we go.

At first, Duke doesn't want to trot. I urge him on. *We've got this far. I know you can do it and so can I, so let's get to it*, I imply with at least some of the fibre of my being, if not all of it. This gives him confidence and he starts to relax, which makes me confident, so I start to relax. Remembering the routine is no problem. I've been reading it on the bus, the train, in my lunch hour, walking it again and again round the kitchen night after night.

Enter at A at walk. At X (which is invisible), take up working trot. At C, track left. From E to B, perform a half 20 m circle left. At B, resume medium walk. From B to E, perform a half 20 m circle left in walk. Between E and K, take up working trot. From K, A to F, continue in working trot. At F, go into medium walk. From B to X, perform a half 10 m circle left, then from X to H perform a half 10 m circle right. This, frankly, is the tricky bit on a big, slightly stiff horse when you're nervous. But we don't do badly. Between H and C, take up working trot. Then, from B to E, perform a half 20

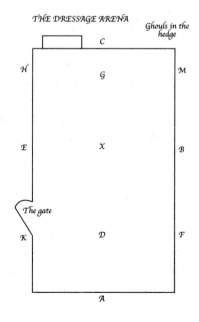

THE DRESSAGE ARENA

Ghouls in the hedge

C

H

G

M

E

X

B

The gate

K

D

F

A

m circle right. At E, go back to medium walk, and between E and B describe a half 20 m circle right, in walk.

The end is in sight. Between F and A, go into working trot, remembering to go into the corners properly to gain extra marks. At A, go down the centre line as straight as you can. At X, go promptly into walk, and at G (G, like X, is unmarked, so you have to guess), halt and salute. Leave the arena, the test paper says, at a free walk on a long rein, or, in my case, in a state of euphoria and relief.

Flick and Tracey have told me repeatedly that my trot must have impulsion. I've got to get Duke working quickly and not shilly-shallying about. They don't say "shilly-shallying" because they are in their twenties and don't sound like characters from a P. G. Wodehouse novel. But I am not and I do. However, I'm a bit cautious about pushing him on while on unknown territory for fear of the consequences, not realizing that this is absolutely the best thing to do as it'll get him concentrating and performing better, gain us more marks, and take his mind off the ghouls in the hedge. It'll also get the test over more quickly.

Instead, I don't push him on and our trot is a bit sloppy, more of a shamble than anything else, but our walk has reasonable impulsion and, if I say it myself, our shapes are lovely. We get neatly into every corner. We describe each shape as well as we can. We even do a nice straight walk down the centre line, which is a whole lot harder than you would think, and manage to halt and salute in the right place.

Flick looks at me slightly grimly. She knows I could have done better. But I didn't totally disgrace myself. My mum, who has no idea what that could and should have looked like, claps furiously. Flick and I stand about chatting to Annie and Kirsten, who've come out as a support team, whilst Duke grazes. Then it's time to head home. Like all return journeys it goes much faster than the outward one. I am now unfazed by the scary objects along the route and the drivers who come haring up behind us, squeal to a near-halt, and then whizz past. By the time we get to the lights I'm quite enjoying myself, despite the fact that we have to stop in traffic and turn right. "These are very quick lights," Flick warns. "We won't have long to get over. So the minute the lights go green, start trotting." I nod. The lights go green and the cars in front pull away. I urge Duke into the kind of trot that he should have been doing at the competition and we fly round the corner one behind the other, with point-gaining impulsion.

"Wheeeeeeeeeeeeeeeee," I scream, like a child on a sledge in winter, as we hurtle along. Flick roars with laughter. And soon we are back on terra firma: Hensting Lane, and the familiar route home.

Then there is a blur of untacking, grooming, feeding and watering, thanking Flick and everyone who helped. And quite suddenly, once again, I don't know how to stand up. So I don't. The test results won't be out until the afternoon, so I drive home, peel off my New Kit, which (including the swanky jacket) is soaked through with sweat, throw it all in the washing machine, and go to bed. It's noon and I sleep like the dead for two hours, which is strange, as I am normally never able to sleep during daylight hours.

When I wake, I think, *That was just five minutes of my life. I shouldn't be this exhausted. I must be far less fit than I thought.* And I didn't think I was fit, whatever the asthma nurse said. But the truth is that I shouldn't be this exhausted. It wasn't that difficult. It was only five minutes. I *am* fit. There is something very, very wrong. I just don't know it yet, or at least I haven't acknowledged it fully. But that horror is for another day.

I get up, put on clean clothes, and drive back to the livery yard to collect my results. The journey to get test results doesn't exist any more. Young people find out the results of their exams online or via text message. But back in the day, when dinosaurs walked the earth and children still took O-Levels, you had to walk to school and peer at a massive board posted outside to find out what you'd got. Then you had to walk home working out what you were going to tell your parents and how you could put a reasonable spin on it. Then you did the same for A-Levels.

And, at degree level, I can vividly remember my abject terror on the day the results were out, knowing that in a few hours' time I could ring the university to find out what I'd got. I was in such a fit of the horrors that by the time I did ring, I couldn't work out what the kind lady at the other end of the phone was saying. "You have an upper second," she said.

"What is that?" I said.

"I've no idea," she said. "But that's what it says here."

"That", said my mother, "is a 2:1. Congratulations!"

The same sense of nausea, of wanting to run away and not know how I've done, comes over me as I drive the few miles to the livery yard. Just like at school, they've posted a sheet of paper with the results on a door. I look for our names. We've got 60 per cent. Sixty per cent! All right, we've come nearly last. But we aren't last. And it was our first time out. I am thrilled.

I scoot back round to the stables where Flick is putting a child and pony through their paces. "We got 60 per cent," I yell, interrupting the lesson. "I can't believe it." And she runs across the thick sandy arena and hugs me over the fence. It is a beginning. Duke also has to be thanked. He, of course, has no idea what all the excitement is about. He's grateful for the extra carrot but, frankly, is just glad to be back in his stable after a day of abnormal exertion. Several small children from the stables also took part. They got higher marks than we did, but even this can't spoil my pleasure. I feel as though we've won a rosette, though we haven't. Oh, how I would love a rosette.

In 2012, now officially besotted with dressage, I will apply for tickets to watch the Olympic dressage competition. Foolishly, I think I have a good chance of getting them, as most people prefer athletics, don't they? Apparently not. The dressage is a sell-out. I am given, instead, tickets for the cross-country day of the three-day-eventing competition. At first I'm gutted. There will be no dancing horses for me. But then Phil and I go to Greenwich Park, tease the service personnel who are doing a fine job of standing in at the last minute for the absent security team, sit in the sun eating and drinking, and just occasionally watch a fabulously competent rider gallop past, not spooking at the crowds, the flags, the jumps, the television cameras, or any of the myriad things that would surely get a horse totally beside itself.

We roar like Romans at the amphitheatre when Zara Tindall enters the arena on her suitably majestic horse, High Kingdom. When the British team gets a silver medal we roar all over again. I also get tickets to see the dressage competition at the Paralympics. Clare and I sit in the pouring rain under a woefully small umbrella, waving patchwork Union Flags that she has made specially, as riders with missing limbs and in some cases no feeling at all in their lower body perform far, far better than I have today. It is breathtaking, inspiring, and joyous. Everyone, I am now completely convinced, can enjoy this horse-riding lark. It doesn't matter how good you are at it. Even if you're rubbish, like me, there is a huge amount of enjoyment to be had. But, my word, if you are good at it, it really must be fun.

October

Everything hurts all the time. Even my bones hurt. How can that be possible? It's not just that my muscles have turned to water, that every step costs me dear, but I'm convinced that my bones actually hurt too. I sleep like the dead and then can barely drag myself out of bed in the morning. The little red dots have gone from my skin, however, and I am going to the toilet less frequently. Perhaps this is what it feels like to get older, I think, I hope. Don't be absurd, says my better self. You are ill.

There isn't time to be sick, however. We are due to fly to Nicaragua for *You Magazine* and Bible Society in a couple of weeks' time. Richard, Ed, Clare, and I are all going but I am the designated Thomas Cook of foreign assignments, so have all the fun of trying to persuade a fixer whom I've never met, who lives on the other side of the world, to prioritize organizing our trip over any other work that she might need to do.

Rebecca (our fixer for Nicaragua) turns out to be utterly fabulous, the kind of person who thinks of every eventuality, plans for it, and understands entirely what we need to do. Rebecca should be cloned and sent ahead of us on every story we ever do. But right now we are having problems communicating with each other, simply because of the time difference and difficulties with languages, email – small things like that. So, as ever in the run-up to a trip, there is a whole load of frustration for me, compounded by the fact that we are still writing up, filing copy, and filling people in on the Ethiopia assignment. So perhaps it's not surprising that I feel as if I'm wading waist-high in treacle, that I could lean against a wall (any wall) and fall asleep for the rest of my life, that everything is far, far too much effort.

But life has to go on and these fleeting weeks between foreign assignments afford me the time, notionally, to spend with my mother, father, cat, and horse. The month starts well as I have what is undoubtedly the best lesson of the year. Flick has not forgotten our lack of impulsion in the dressage test and is setting about fixing that failing once and for all. We spend half an hour in the outdoor arena, with her thinking of curious ways to engage my mind. Flick's tip for gaining impulsion but controlling speed is this: "Imagine that you are trying to crack a nut between your shoulder blades. Now stay like that." To get Duke really listening, what she calls "between hand and leg", I must do different speeds in trot, whilst concentrating on cracking the aforementioned nut. And it works! He lifts himself up through his capacious rear end, works through his back, and really genuinely moves. No, he floats. He is a different horse. Flick is cheering. I am slack-jawed in disbelief.

After our lesson, Duke and I head down the road by ourselves, cracking nuts the entire way. Duke, who normally plods stoically along, as if bearing a heavy sack of potatoes, now glides down the lane, brain in gear, backside in gear, listening to me, floating, self-consciously fabulous. I have never been more proud of him and I'm fairly delighted with myself too.

The next day we do it again. Annie is looking for company on a ride, not because she wants to chat, but because Lady is carrying an injury. My job is to ride behind them commenting all the way on Lady's way-of-going, or, as we say in English, how the horse is moving. I do a running commentary on Lady's stiffness and, as a consequence, entirely forget to be nervous, and so relax and enjoy the whole thing. I also forget to crack the nut at any stage of the ride, but you can't have everything, can you?

My neighbour, Steve, has two apple trees that are heavily laden this autumn, and he regularly brings buckets of unwanted fruit to me. I have made juice, mint jelly, chutney, dried apple rings, and baked apples, and cooked more stewed apple than you could ever wish to eat, so now it is the horses' turn. For being good two days in a row, Duke gets six apples. If a horse could smile, he would.

There are other lovely moments too. My mother is now sufficiently recovered to be able to go out in company. Always fans of church fêtes, we go to the autumn fayre organized by her village church. We buy things we don't need, simply for the pleasure of being able to support the church, and sit around in late-autumn sunshine with lots of other villagers, eating a scratch lunch that the local ladies have provided. I can't recall attending such a convivial, relaxed church affair since I was a child. Then, church fêtes were about as exciting as life got. And in the days before eBay and car-boot sales, they were the places to offload things you no longer wanted, and buy things that others were passing on. They were also very, very good for cakes.

At our village chapel there was an unwritten rule that if you helped out on a stall you got first dibs of the wares. This was infuriating for the people who queued round the common to get in first. But it made sense to us. After all, we'd been there sorting old pairs of trousers since the early morning. As a child, this was where I bought everyone's Christmas presents. I didn't have much money. Actually, neither did my parents, so we seldom went shopping. But the cakes were the great thing. The women of our village knew how to bake; they could have given Mary Berry a run for her money. There were cakes of every flavour known to man, small, large, and multi-layered cakes, and, for children like me, paper plates laden with fairy cakes. I'd always buy them, and my mother (who was an excellent baker herself) would invariably indulge in a cake that someone else had made. There were few greater childhood pleasures than being allowed to help choose the cake that we would take home.

So we know a thing or two about fêtes, my mum and I. And we definitely know the difference between a good one and a bad one. We've been to both, though we haven't stayed at the bad ones for long. Good fêtes must have the following elements: an excellent cake stall; wearable second-hand clothing; a book stall where paperback books cost no more than 50p and hardbacks top out at £1; a bottle stall where you always win something, generally a decent bottle of red wine; a plant stall that has such variety at low prices that you could plant a whole garden from it; a human fruit machine; splat-the-rat; someone selling unwanted champagne flutes; the chance to win a hamper of food; a toy stall, and finally a fruit and vegetable stall with plenty of marrows. There must always, always, be a slightly less noisy place to sit down and have a fearsomely strong cup of tea (served in a bone china cup and saucer) and a ubiquitous, compulsory slice of cake (served on a bone china plate).

A bad fête has about half a dozen stalls, all of which are run by people whose mind isn't on the job and never has been; where you are charged £2 for admission, and where there isn't a cup of tea or a slice of cake. You must eschew these events and walk away; they are not worthy of the name "fête". But the Twyford Church autumn fayre is a pukka event. There are some serious bakers among the local women, and the fabulous Betty New from the neighbouring village of Morestead has been called in to make meringues. These are the size of Duke's hooves, ladled with thick cream, and then, just in case you hadn't got enough sugar inside you, another meringue is added to create a cream sandwich. There are few things I wouldn't do for one of Betty's meringues.

There is no point in taking Daddy. He would find it bewildering. But I do take him out to Fran's kitchen garden, where we all pick runner beans. He's a bit confused, but at least he's in a garden, using his hands, which are becoming paper-pale and translucent through lack of hard work, sun, and wind.

So everything appears to be going swimmingly, if you ignore the aching pain, the headaches, the exhaustion, and the incipient panic about whether or not the Nicaragua trip will come together – which I do. Then an old magazine pal rings me. She's editing a monthly title in London. Can I come up and help for a few days, as they're short-staffed and hurtling at speed towards deadline? She's the person who first inspired my interest in foreign news, so I am delighted to oblige.

Going to London used to be a breeze. Now it tires me more. This time, on the last evening, I barely know how to put one foot in front of the other as I walk to the Tube. I have to force myself to concentrate on lifting my left foot and putting it down, then lifting my right foot and putting that down, over and over, slowly, painfully slowly. People flow past me to the right and left. They seem to be going so fast. It is as if I am moving in slow motion. There are just four days to go before we head to Nicaragua. I finally recognize that I am genuinely not well. If I struggle to walk to the Tube, how will I cope with two weeks in Latin America? The answer, quite obviously, is that I won't.

I seek a diagnosis: the first of many, it transpires. On a Saturday morning this means seeing a tired, stressed young doctor at a walk-in clinic at the local hospital. I tell my sorry tale: Ethiopia, mosquito bite, diarrhoea, headaches, bone-aching weariness, sweating, and the inability to stand or walk. "You have had", he says, "a urinary tract infection." He gives me some tablets that should clear it up in five days. Five days? I'm meant to be on a plane in four. Five days, he says. I put my flight back a day and tell Richard, Ed, and Clare that I'll meet them there. I try walking back from the hospital across town. I can't do it. I have to sit down on a bench and wait until I can breathe properly. Then I call a cab. When I'm safely home and the door is shut, I howl and weep with frustration, and rage against the unspeakable, unknowable illness that is overwhelming me. What is wrong?

Certainly not a urinary tract infection, that's for sure. I may as well be eating Smarties, for all the good the tablets do. The days tick by. The others pack and get ready to fly out to Nicaragua, and I am no better. If anything, I'm worse. When I stand up or walk, I feel light-headed and weak; everything spins round. I need to see a GP. Any GP. I'd be hard-pressed to see my own, utterly fabulous, doctor at this juncture. She's way too popular and brilliant. To be honest, everyone's fabulous, and appointments are hard to come by. "It might be vertigo," says the NHS Direct staff member whom I call. "You need to see a GP." Yeah, right, because that's been really easy to arrange thus far, hasn't it?

My flights are still booked and I'm determined to go. The day before the flight I'm sitting in the garden, drinking a cup of tea. When it's time to go inside, I stand up and very slowly, very gracefully (I like to think), collapse onto the garden bench. After this comes a lot of crying, with the realization that I cannot possibly go to Nicaragua. I've never been to Latin America, and I'm not going now. Everyone is very kind, but I am devastated. I feel that I'm letting the team down. I am letting myself down too. There is work to be done and I am not doing it. How can I explain that away? But, deep in my spirit, I am frightened about what's happening to me.

No one seems to know what's wrong. I consult a series of

doctors and we play a medical version of "pin the tail on the donkey". Each one says something different. None of them, as it turns out, is right. And why would they be? There can't be too many cases of Horrid Tropical Diseases in leafy Hampshire. Finally, it is decided that I must go for tests at the hospital to find out exactly what is wrong. I take a number and wait for the day to dawn.

It ultimately does and I drag myself to the hospital and wait some more. I am so tired and in so much pain that I don't know how to sit in the waiting room. After what seems an interminable amount of time, a kindly nurse realizes that I am fading fast and brings pillows to prop me up. Regardless of what anyone in the waiting room thinks of me, I curl up in the chair and long for oblivion. I wait some more. Finally, it's my turn. I explain: Ethiopia, mosquito, headaches, diarrhoea, bone-aching weariness, no chance of going to Nicaragua.

"Did you have a rash?" says the doctor.

"A rash? No," I say, "but I did have these strange little red dots all over me." Everyone looks at me very hard. That was a rash, you idiot, their silence implies. There are whispered consultations. People go in and out of the room without making eye contact with me. The kind nurse brings the pillows in. Then they start taking blood. They take so much that I'm concerned I won't have any left. No one will tell me what it is, what they suspect, but they definitely suspect something and, whatever it is, it isn't good. "We'll contact your GP," they say. "We'll let you know."

I take to my bed. I don't want to sound too much like a melodramatic character in a Victorian novel, but there's nothing for it. Standing up, walking around, thinking, writing: I can't do any of them. So I lie in bed day after day with occasional ventures downstairs to feed George-the-cat and the chickens, and perhaps make a cup of tea. Time passes very slowly. I become familiar with all the cracks in my bedroom ceiling. There are plenty of them. And all the spiders that have come indoors to escape the early-autumn chill. There are a decent number of them too, but thankfully George likes to chase them away, and sometimes eats the larger ones.

A friend who works in medicine rings me with some advice on how to recover: divide your time, she says, into five-minute blocks. First do five minutes of something physical. No, this does not include horse riding. It might mean laying the fire, or getting dressed, or hanging out some washing. After that, do five minutes of something that uses your brain, for example, reading. Don't try writing just yet, she warns. Then, after you've done that for ten minutes, you will be pooped. She doesn't say "pooped" because she's a proper medical type, but that's what she means. So then, she says, you have five minutes' rest, which in your case, Hazel, means lying quietly on your bed without trying to read or listen to Radio 4. These three things will give you balance, she says. And balance is what you very badly need.

"How long does this go on?" I ask. She doesn't exactly answer, but what she does say is that I have to go on doing the five-minute routine each day until it becomes easy. Then I can do six minutes, and so on. This will obviously be very, very slow indeed. But it will work. There are some inevitable consequences of dividing your time into five-minute blocks. First, it takes a whole day of physical five-minute slots to prepare one meal, which you eat in the evening. Second, your house and garden become very messy. So do you. Third, you cannot leave the house. And, fourth, it means you cannot see your loan horse. As it takes twenty minutes on a good day with a following wind to drive to the stables, it will be weeks before I've built up enough five-minute slots to drive there and back, let alone see Duke too. If I had the energy, I would cry.

Duke has got me through the first nine months of this wretched year, and now I can't see him to help me struggle through the last three months. I am bereft. Worse, I know that it cannot be explained to him that I am ill and he will just think that I've abandoned him and don't care any more. That, too, is hard to bear. The tables are turning. I don't simply look to Duke for support; I want to support him too. I want him to know that he is loved, appreciated, and valued, and not just a hard-working animal doing the bidding of humans. I want to make a positive difference to his life, as he has done to mine. But I can't, because I am bed-bound.

While I wait to find out what kind of tropical disease I have, for undoubtedly it must be that, both Duke and George fall ill too. First, it's Duke. Flick calls from the yard to say that he's gone lame. Duke has long had problems with a tiny bone in his front feet called the navicular bone. There are, as I understand it, lots of different reasons why this could be: the bone itself could be crumbling; the surrounding tendons could be weakening; the bone could have developed lesions; or the ligaments could be calcified. We don't know. What we do know is that "navicular", as it's commonly termed, causes lameness. Any one of these things (or perhaps all of them) happen, it causes strain and pain, and he ends up hopping around the field with very hurty front feet. He will recover, but like any injury it needs rest. I am beside myself with worry about him. In fact, I am more worried about him than I am about my own health, because I am powerless to get to the yard and tend to his needs, should I even know what those needs might be. I can't give him a comforting stroke and a carrot and tell him that one day soon his feet will be all right again. They will stop hurting.

I picture him standing in a field by himself as all his pals go in to do their day's work, lonely, in pain, and looking for me. Of course, he has a whole team of professional people to look after him and thus will be fine, but that isn't part of my morose little imagining. Annie and Kirsten ring to tell me that Duke is indeed fine and that they are giving him apples. Feeling low in spirits, I imagine the worst. I think that they are just trying to cheer me up and that he isn't all right at all. I wait for Flick to ring and say that, actually, he's not going to get better, and that this is the end of the road for Duke. Days pass slowly and the call doesn't come. Somehow that doesn't make me more hopeful; it simply makes me anxious that it is still ahead.

Then, early one morning, George-the-cat jumps up onto the bed, purring loudly, in his daily bid to get me up and feeding him. He has learned through long years of experience that the best way to make me move is to purr and be friendly, rather than yowl and be impatient. He purrs and purrs. I stroke him with my eyes shut. He purrs some more. I open one eye and sit bolt upright in bed. He is sitting holding his right paw up for inspection. He can't put any weight on it. He can't walk on it. How he got into the house, up the stairs, and onto the bed with an injured paw is beyond me. I carry him down to the kitchen and he tries to eat, but keeps toppling forward into his bowl. I call the vet. "Bring him round," she says.

I use up several days' worth of physical five-minute slots driving to the vet's, waiting, and then explaining the paw-waving incident. George needs to have his paw X-rayed. So he is sedated and the X-ray is done. It is best, we are told, not to see how laws or sausages are made. I'd add to that list how your cat responds to medical care when in pain. The vet is fantastic, but George (normally placid and sociable) is definitely in pain. "This makes him Very Angry With Us," says the vet, euphemistically. You can imagine how cross a 7 kg cat can be – even a cat with only three working legs. He still has teeth and claws, and he can of course hiss, swear, and curse. He does all three.

The vet brings him back in, trying to look as if it's been a straightforward process. George has broken a bone in his paw. There's a theme here: Duke can't stand up, George can't stand up, and neither can I. The vet has put a cast on George's leg and one of those upside-down-lampshade things round his neck to stop him licking his plaster off. They've tried to improve the plaster by making it pink with blue spots. I'm not entirely sure it works, but it's a kind thought.

Every evening George is to have painkillers in some tuna. He is not allowed upstairs or indeed outdoors. I must install a litter tray and he will have to sleep on the sofa, as he can't walk about on a broken paw. You try telling George that. Every evening I limp downstairs, mix drugs into his tuna, and then watch while he goes completely cross-eyed, his pupils like saucers, rocking and swaying as the painkillers take hold of him. Then, the idea goes, he will be so tired that he'll just fall asleep on the sofa and snooze right through until morning.

This doesn't take into consideration that George, like any cat, is a creature of habit. Since I rescued him six years ago, he has spent every night of his life sleeping at the end of my bed. He is not a cuddly cat, snuggling up close, but he likes to be in the vicinity of a friendly stroke, so the end of the bed is his place. He is not going to let little things like being unable to walk or being doped out of his head stop him from walking upstairs and trying to get on the bed. At first, I take him back down and put him on the sofa, as sagely instructed by the vet. But the piteous result of this is that he just attempts the stairs again. So in the end I carry him up and put him on the end of the bed, and hope that it won't slow his recovery.

It is very, very difficult to get a good night's sleep when you are sharing a bed with a cat with a broken foot who is determined to spend half the night trying to lick his plaster off and the other half having crazy, drug-induced dreams. But as I am doing very little with myself during the day, this hardly matters. I can catch up on my sleep then. I do.

Six weeks pass. Every week George has to return to the vet, which he views with increasing horror and distaste as time goes on, as he knows what to expect. Each week he is sedated and has an X-ray and his cast is changed. We continue with the druggy-tuna routine. He is trying his best to walk on his bad leg, but can't go outside, so he sleeps, and time slowly heals his foot. The day comes when the last plaster can be taken off and he is allowed to go free. His injured leg has withered, through lack of activity, to half the size of his other ones. It is a feeble sight. But eventually, the vet assures me, the fur will regrow and muscle will build up. But it will take a while.

Flick rings. I hold my breath. "Duke is better," she says. "He's doing some work, just in walk. We don't want to get him trotting yet in case it jars his front feet and sets him back. But he's up and about and off the sick list." I am overjoyed and relieved. And still in bed. My time slots, however, are getting longer. I'm up to twenty minutes of activity at one time, which is real progress. But I need to be able to do at least an hour if I'm going to be able to drive to the yard, groom Duke, and return home. Who knew you could miss a horse at all, let alone this badly?

Not only am I unable to visit Duke, I can't yet string enough minutes together to visit either of my parents. There are many reasons for feeling bad about this. But chief among them is that it means my mother has to visit my father alone and unsupported, something that she finds draining and upsetting. The man she sits with is not the man she married, and hasn't been for a long while. It's just six months since she had her stroke and any emotional upset sets her recovery back. Neither is she robust yet. So visiting Daddy is harder now than it would have been if she were well and strong. But there's nothing for it. If visiting Duke involves a one-hour physical time slot, visiting my dad will involve ninety minutes. I am a long way from that yet.

Towards the end of the month, I unexpectedly receive a letter from the consultant microbiologist at the hospital. I say unexpectedly, because somehow, in the fog of my brain, I'd anticipated that he would contact my GP and I would be summoned to see her and hear all about it. Instead of which, along with a copy of *The Radio Times*, a few charity appeal letters, and a phone bill, I receive a letter that takes my breath away.

"The reference laboratory has returned results which show that you have antibodies to dengue fever, West Nile virus, tick-borne encephalitis virus, and yellow fever," the consultant microbiologist writes. "There is nothing specific that needs to be done about these results apart from noting that it is possible that your recent illness could have been due to dengue."

I sit down hard on the chair in the kitchen where George normally waits for his tea. It is known as the Waiting Chair. I am round-eyed and open-mouthed. What a list. No wonder I feel ill. I read and reread the letter, but with my brain still only on twenty-minute sessions (and this not being one of them) I can't make much of it. Thankfully, Phil is coming to visit this weekend and cheer up the patient, so I resolve to ask him what the letter means.

When Phil turns up everything within me wants to thrust the letter at him and say, "Look at this! I have everything in the tropical medical handbook. What is going on?" But I don't, because he's just driven for an hour in Friday-night traffic, having worked hard all week. I've been stockpiling my physical twenty-minute slots (which my other medical pal would, I'm sure, tell me is not how it's meant to work) in order to cook dinner.

On the menu tonight is roast muntjac deer. Phil and I are huge fans of game, having a couple of chums who sell game for a living and who have become so used to being surrounded by dead pheasants that they generously force a brace on us whenever they see us. Once we realized how delicious pheasant was (and George-the-cat concurred and purred at the resulting titbits he was given), we branched out into other game: roast partridge and guinea fowl; rabbit cooked in cider; diced venison made into a stew; home-made game pie; and, my particular favourite, haunch of muntjac deer.

These russet-coloured deer are small, standing at just four feet high. The males have little four-inch antlers. They have angular, pointed faces that look for all the world like something on a Chinese vase. There's a reason for this, as they were first brought to the UK from China as recently as the twentieth century. Their first home was Woburn Park in Bedfordshire. But deer get around, and, ultimately, deliberate releases from Woburn, Northamptonshire, and Warwickshire led to the establishment of feral populations. They have a strange barking call and like living in woodland, but are increasingly to be found in people's back gardens – decent-sized back gardens akin to grounds, one assumes, as they are not yet in mine.

And they taste delicious.

A leg of muntjac deer is as easy to cook as a leg of lamb (I use the same recipe), and this has become my absolute standby dish of the day. Tonight, we are having roast muntjac deer with roast vegetables, an array of green vegetables, and very, very thick gravy, and then, because I will be all out of twenty-minute slots in which to prepare any more food, cheese and fruit. So we have this and all three of us relax. Yes, George eats muntjac deer too: no pouches of hard-to-recognize cat food for him. I know what goes into his dish. There are no E-numbers. And when we're all quite smiley and chirpy, I produce the letter.

"Oh my," says Phil, which is an unusually strong reaction from him. "Let me read that again." He reads the letter in full several times. Then he looks at me. "No wonder you feel ill," he says.

Joking aside, he picks through the consultant microbiologist's meaning. "First, let's take yellow fever," he says. "You've been inoculated against that. Hence you have antibodies in your blood. That's where that one comes from. Now, let's take tick-borne encephalitis." "You can die of that," I say. "Yes, I know," he says. "But you haven't. So let's keep some perspective. I think that this must have been what you had a couple of years ago when you had meningitis."

I'd been on a reporting trip to Jordan and had returned with some cold-like virus picked up from a pal at the BBC, which after a fortnight had decided that being in my nose and throat wasn't a sufficient adventure, and moved on to my spinal cord and brain fluid. That was a laugh. Meningitis. You get to hospital quickly in an ambulance if you've got that. I have only vague memories of it: being unable to bear the light and a wise paramedic covering my head with a blanket; trying to get out of the light in the general medical ward and curling up in a ball; a student nurse doing a lumbar puncture on my back with me growling in pain, hissing at the doctor who told me to stop crying; falling out of bed; and Phil coming the next day to take me home. "Hospital is no place for the sick," he'd said. So that, he now deduced, had actually been tick-borne encephalitis.

The idea of having meningitis was bad enough, but somehow tick-borne encephalitis is worse. Decades before, I'd known someone who had got it and they had been ill and bedridden for years. And they were a lot, lot younger than I am now. But the symptoms were all there: confusion, disorientation, sensitivity to bright light, and an inability to speak. That'll teach me to go yomping about through beautiful Jordanian meadows without watching out for ticks.

"So," says Phil, returning to the Letter of Infinite Peril. "That leads us on nicely to dengue fever and West Nile virus. You must have just had both of those, which would explain why it's taking you a long while to get better." Phil has made me promise, solemnly, on all that I hold dear, that I will never, ever Google any physical symptoms that I experience. But there are, it would seem, professional medical and pharmaceutical websites that he knows about. So we look at those and suck our teeth at the symptoms.

West Nile virus is, like so many things, a flu-like virus. You may get a headache, muscle aches (you betcha), and a fever. A few people, like me, get it really badly, and that can mean the meningitis symptoms, muscle weakness, and loss of consciousness. That would explain collapsing on the plane and during the cab ride home from Heathrow, then.

West Nile virus is the nicer of the two illnesses. Dengue fever is a whole lot worse. You will have a fever, severe headache, pain behind the eyes, muscle and joint pain, nausea or vomiting, and swollen glands. You may also have a rash, which would explain the red dots on my skin. You will be very, very tired, the specialist websites say, and it will take a goodish while to recover. But there are things I'm yet to discover about Dengue fever that will really frighten me.

Phil and I sit, muntjac deer forgotten, looking at this brief letter that explains what's wrong with me. All the laughter and jollity have gone out of the evening. Phil shakes his head. "No wonder you feel ill," he says again. "You must promise me that you will never travel abroad again."

I swallow hard. I have been to more than thirty countries

with my work. I love meeting people from so many different cultures and backgrounds, listening to their stories, and finding, repeatedly, that we are all the same: there is so much more that unites us than separates us. I pride myself on being willing to get on any plane, going anywhere. If a commissioning editor rings up and says, "Will you go to Outer Mongolia?", I will go.

The only foreign trip I've ever turned down was when I was offered the chance to do the Cresta Run. The Cresta Run is the home of the St Moritz Tobogganing Club, founded in 1844/5. This makes it sound terribly jolly, but to me it is the last word in absolutely terrifying. The Cresta Run is a natural ice run, built from scratch every year with snow that is then iced. It starts at St Moritz and winds its way down the valley to what used to be the village of Cresta. It's about three-quarters of a mile long and drops 514 feet, and its gradient varies from 1 in 2.8 to 1 in 8.7. And you do this lying flat on the modern equivalent of a tea tray.

So when I had a call a few years ago to ask if I wanted to go, I turned it down flat. If I don't like getting above a trot on a horse, I can't see me enjoying whizzing down a near-ice tunnel on a tea tray wearing Lycra. Can you? But not go abroad at all? What would I do? Who would I be? How would I earn a living? Would anything ever be as interesting again?

But I can see why Phil is suggesting this. "Soon," he says, trying to inject a bit of levity back into the proceedings, "it'll be more dangerous for a mosquito to bite you than for you to be bitten by it." But we both know that it's not really that funny and some difficult choices lie ahead.

November

Convalescence is slow. If you are well, it sounds appealing: sleeping for long periods of time, watching box sets of DVDs, drinking tea, and eating as healthily as you can, whilst, crucially, avoiding work. This would be fine for one day, but for weeks on end, with no sense of when you will feel sufficiently well to do anything else, it is no fun at all. It is made worse by the isolation that comes with it, which in my case leads to worry. I worry about not just *when* I will recover, but *whether* I will. Furthermore, will I be well enough to work again? Right now, I can't imagine having the strength to get to a news story, let alone the wit to interview people and write the copy up to a deadline. And if I can't work, what will happen to me, Duke, the house, and George-the-cat? In the small hours of the night, I lie awake running through grim sets of worst-case scenarios. What is it about 4 a.m. that does not readily conjure up happy images of recovery, health, and happiness?

For many years I'd worked the religious affairs beat, pitching news stories on that subject to a variety of papers, though my happiest hunting ground has always been *The Telegraph*. There was a small, dwindling coterie of religious affairs reporters who worked for a range of national newspapers and the BBC. We had known each other for years and were on good terms. Unlike some newsrooms, which can be competitive places, sitting with this group filing copy was always refreshing. It felt like being in the company of both old friends and long-term colleagues simultaneously. Generally, people shared what they had discovered, passing on quotes that might have given them an exclusive story. If someone was confused about what the top-line, or gist, of the story was, another journalist would explain it. There was a sense of collaboration about the work that went on there. As a group, they shared each other's successes and misfortunes. There were few egos, and those there were were tolerated.

Now, I am watching them all reporting from outside St Paul's Cathedral from the dull comfort of my sofa. An anti-capitalist movement, known as Occupy London, had been heading for the London Stock Exchange but, finding their way barred, had set up camp – quite literally – outside St Paul's Cathedral. It was suddenly all go for religious affairs reporters: Cinderella was going to the ball. First, the Dean of the Cathedral declared that St Paul's would close its doors. It did. Then a week later, it reopened. The Canon Chancellor, Dr Giles Fraser, a cleric skilled in communicating through the media, resigned. This was, he said, because, "I believe that the Chapter has set on a course of action that could mean that there will be violence in the name of the Church".

I should be there. I would normally be there. But I am not. Instead, night after night I watch Robert Pigott, currently the BBC's religious affairs correspondent, setting the news agenda for the day, kicking off bulletins, reporting live from the encampment outside St Paul's. I wonder if the journalist within me has withered and died, as nothing stirs in my soul. Normally, I would be racing out of the door, notepad in hand, seeking out interviews myself, trying to add something to the sum of the reporting being done. I'd be there with the pack, as so often before. Now, I don't even have the energy to care that I'm not at the biggest news story to hit the church in a goodish long while. If I hadn't known it before, this is when I realize that something is profoundly wrong with me.

I always wanted to be a journalist. All right, to be absolutely accurate, there were a few years before this realization dawned. We'll call those years childhood. Then, in 1976, when I was just twelve years old, Alan J. Pakula directed the film *All the President's Men,* and the course of my life was set. The film starred Robert Redford and Dustin Hoffman as the real-life reporters Woodward and Bernstein from *The Washington Post* and told the story of Watergate: the slow unravelling of the powerbase around, and the fall of, President Nixon. For reasons that no one can remember, when it was aired on British television, I was allowed to stay up and watch it.

I was mesmerized. Two journalists kept picking away at loose ends of stories that didn't seem to make sense, continuing to ask questions, even at risk to their lives, when the whole news agenda was against them; and from that doggedness something extraordinary arose. It wasn't the glamour that appealed to me; it wasn't glamorous. Strangely, people always think that journalism is glamorous. It's not. It's very, very hard work in unsocial hours, days, weeks, and months, and, in the case of the Watergate journalists, years. But I'd been warned about this, aged twelve. Because what drew me to journalism in this film was the idea of hard graft: working away at something until it comes right; of digging under beds for bones; of finding something out and telling people about it.

There was seemingly no way that a teenage girl in a rural backwater in England could make the leap into journalism. I knew no one in the trade who could offer me a helping hand. Worse, few wanted to encourage me, journalists at that time having about the same social status as tax collectors and prostitutes in the Bible. Teachers at my smart grammar school were appalled by the notion that I wanted to become a reporter. The highest-achieving girls (of which I definitely was not one) wanted to be doctors, accountants, vets, and lawyers. By wanting to be a Fleet Street hack, I was letting the side down.

My friends thought it was an unachievable ambition. Even my mother was far from convinced, though she came to be the perfect mother-of-a-hack, knowing the best rate for every story, what made both a strong national news story and a feature, and what behaviour from newsdesks could be deemed acceptable and what could not. But back then, my sole encourager was the Reverend Hedley Feast, the minister of the Baptist chapel, who, in his spare time, filed football match reports for BBC Radio Oxford. He believed it was possible that I could do this, and so opened the door a crack into a world of words and news.

Ignorance was my major problem. I knew I wanted to be a reporter, but didn't know how. I had no idea what made a news story, how to construct it, how papers worked, who took what stories from whom, and how on earth you went about getting into the trade. So I made many mistakes and took a long time to learn. But, along the way, there were just enough people to fan the flames of my desire to report to keep me going. *The Sunday Times'* Peter and Leni Gillman and the BBC's Justin Phillips were my chief cheerleaders, and I owe them a huge debt of thanks.

By the time I was in my late twenties, I was permanently running after stories, ears pricked for even the suggestion that something reportable was about to happen. I went on dates with my reporter's notepad, contacts book, and mobile phone in my handbag, in case something interesting happened on the way there. (It certainly didn't always happen while I was on the date!) I carried my passport with me at all times, lest someone – anyone – might want to send me abroad on a story. I worked constantly and loved it. A normal week would see me putting in between eighty and a hundred hours' work. So there had never been a moment, until now, when I had looked at a news story breaking and not wished, with every fibre of my being, that I was there too.

But illness does this to you. Your mind, my medical pal tells me, is the last thing to recover. Your body has to get well first, so your brain seemingly shuts down in order to let it do so. Once your body is healed, your mind will follow, she says. I sit on the sofa watching the news, and trust that she is right.

Phil always says that life is about the management of expectations. In this case, the expectations are about convalescence. It's not something that we consider necessary these days. If you have the misfortune to go to hospital, you're sent home as quickly as possible. If you have a cough-cold-flu bug, you stagger into work feigning heroism and say, "It's OK; I can struggle on," whilst passing your germs to the rest of the office.

Back in Victorian times, they knew a thing or two about convalescence. They knew that home is not necessarily the most restful place to be when you are sick. It might be teeming with small, noisy children. It might be cold, draughty, or, at the very least, full of things you feel you should be doing. So, if you were middle-class during the Victorian era, it was *de rigueur* to spend time at a convalescent home after an illness. I quite fancy that now: somewhere with no television or newspapers to remind me of what I'm missing; no computer, so that I am not drawn to email; and a place where meals magically appear three times a day. Surely that has to be better for you than sitting on the sofa watching DVDs and eating rubbish?

Sadly, convalescent homes are, like branch lines on the railway network, a thing of the past. So there is nothing for it but to continue to build up my blocks of time from twenty minutes to twenty-five, and so on, painfully and slowly. Of course, if I actually lived in the fictional world that my journalist pals like to believe I do – that of a large house on its own landed estate – being unwell would not represent a problem. I would have staff to tend to my needs, a cook to rustle up calf's foot jelly, and a groom to bring Duke to the door, so that, at the very least, I could stroke his ears and give him a carrot. This, I have to say, is an appealing notion.

However, my recovery from the mixed lurgy of Ethiopia is less *Downton Abbey* and more *Strictly Come Dancing*: two steps forward, one step back.

Some days I feel that I'm improving and set about doing something ambitious, such as, say, half an hour of gardening, and then the next day I pay for it, sinking back, exhausted, onto the sofa. There are no sequins in my shimmy, but what you can say about it is that it is regular and predictable. If I have a couple of over-active days, they will without doubt be followed by a day when I feel as if I am entirely made of water. These days are less of a "Ten from Len" and more of a "Dis*a*ster, darling" from Craig.

There is a lovely story – referenced in Jim Kirkwood's book *There Must Be a Pony* – about a father who has two sons. One's an optimist, the other a pessimist. At Christmas, the father thinks he'll try a bit of an experiment and gives masses of presents to the pessimistic son. He spots the boy in his bedroom looking at the mound of gifts, trying to work out what the catch is. To the optimistic son he gives an awful lot of manure. Instead of being upset that this is his Christmas gift, the lad eagerly starts shovelling the stuff up. His father asks him why he is so happy, and he replies, "With all this horse dung, there must be a pony."

I am by nature the pessimistic child, but I reckon that, given my situation, I should take the view of the optimistic child. If I keep shovelling my five-minute blocks of time for long enough and keep going despite setbacks, there will be a pony at the end of it. Or, to be more precise, there will be Duke. Annie and Kirsten visit, bringing with them vitality, energy, enthusiasm, and tales of horse riding. They cross their fingers behind their backs and tell me that Duke is absolutely fine: missing me, obviously, but doing just dandy, feet not hurting, mud not affecting his legs, not working too hard, and so on. They tell stories of recent rides, dressage competitions, what everyone else at the yard is doing. We drink tea and I listen. Slowly I start to fade. I stop talking. In the end, I'm just a physical presence. Even listening is tiring. We'll call this a one-step-backwards day.

There are two-steps-forward days as well. The first of these comes when I've built up enough blocks of time to drive myself to the water meadows five minutes away, and walk for twenty minutes to the St Cross Hospital. Don't imagine a modern hospital. Picture instead an ancient church with almshouses standing alongside a river. Think *Wolf Hall* or even *Brother Cadfael*, and you've about got it. It is one of my favourite places in Winchester, as it is invariably tranquil and restorative.

How the place began is shrouded in mystery, but there's a good story about what might have happened, which goes like this. When Henry of Blois (the grandson of William the Conqueror and, coincidentally, the Bishop of Winchester) was walking through the water meadows, he met a local girl who begged him to help the people who were starving because of the civil war. As he continued on his walk he came upon a ruined religious house and decided to reinstate it to help the local community, as the girl had asked. Who knows if it's true? But what is known is that the Hospital of St Cross was founded between 1132 and 1136 and is the oldest charitable institution in England. And surely it's one of the most beautiful too.

As for the story, my money is on it being apocryphal. The bitter civil war between Henry I's daughter, Empress Maud (also known as Matilda), and his nephew, King Stephen, raged from 1135 until 1154. During this time, Bishop Henry swapped sides at least three times, and ultimately set fire to Winchester during the siege of that city in 1141. So my guess is that he had other things to do than wander in the nearby water meadows and listen to starving young women. But I could be wrong.

Either way, the walled garden at St Cross Hospital contains mighty old trees and fabulous herbaceous borders. The church is still well attended and twenty-four "brothers" live in the amazing almshouses. They're not monks. They're just ordinary blokes who are spending their declining years in splendour. One of my friends, quite sensibly, has his name on the list. To live there, you have to be over retirement age, in need, able to look after yourself (this is not a very posh care home), and willing to wear the gown and hat of the "brothers" in public. And, frankly, who wouldn't, if it meant living there?

A road cuts through the water meadows. I park there and walk, shakily, along the broad path towards St Cross Hospital. I've loved it since I first stumbled upon it nearly twenty-five years ago, and I love it still. If I am going to feel better anywhere, it will be here. But just the walk is uplifting. I feel like a prisoner released from jail. Putting one foot in front of the other; looking at the sky; seeing the trees in their last throes of autumn glory; hearing the river run gently past: all feel like life's richest possible blessings. Back in my fit-as-a-fiddle days, I used to run along here three times a week. Now, I plod slowly. As ever, I don't have much impulsion, but at least I'm moving.

Finally, I get to the gate that leads to the hospital. I walk through the field that surrounds it, where cows are grazing, and beyond I can see swans on the river. Back in Henry of Blois' day it was possible for all passing pilgrims en route to Canterbury to beg the wayfarer's dole here: bread and beer. As a nod to this caring, hospitable past, the hospital still gives out a token reminder of the dole to this day: a small piece of bread and a sip of beer. It is enough, on this mild autumnal day, to restore me. I sit in the quadrangle looking at the church, feeling closer to the ancient past than to the present. St Cross Hospital seems to me to be what Anglicans would call "a thin place", a place where you can reach out and touch something divine. But, more than that, it seems to have a thinness with the past. The footsteps and prayers of the pilgrims of the past echo loudly here.

Thus restored, I plan my next outing whenever a two-steps-forward day should come my way. It's my father's birthday, so cards, cakes, gifts, and flowers are assembled. I use up a full day's energy on this because it is a bittersweet occasion. Every birthday is joyous, but this one is tinged with sadness because it's his first in care, and because Daddy is struggling to understand what is going on.

He's pleased to see us; pleased too with the gifts, flowers, and cake. The amazingly productive cook at the care home bakes a second enormous cake, which will allow everyone who lives in my dad's slightly demented wing in the home to have a slice. Tea and cake are served. It's as jolly as it can be – which is not very jolly at all. My father only wants to talk about when he can come home. "Why am I in prison?" he says.

"Why are you keeping me in captivity?"

"I want to come home."

"When am I coming home?"

I explain yet again that Mummy has had a stroke and needs to rest; that the doctors think it would be better if he stays here for now. He disagrees. Furiously. Every time we have this conversation, it's the same. Awful. It's bad enough having to talk about this once, but repeatedly at every visit is soul-wrenching for us all. I wish that he could remember and understand, but he can't and this is not about to change. These conversations will go on until he loses the power of speech, which will come, though mercifully none of us knows that yet. We'll call this a three-or-four-steps-back day.

My progress this month looks like an erratic medical chart: full of ups and downs, but generally heading in the right direction. I am focused on one thing alone: not returning to work (I can't yet imagine being able to write), but returning to Duke's side. I have not been there during his lameness. He has not had my moral or physical support. If I have a reason to get better, it is to see him again and to nurture his soul as he limps through pain, hopefully to full health again. Time passes. Finally, I have accrued enough time to drive to the yard and groom Duke for ten minutes, sit down, and, later, when strength has returned, drive home again.

I'm not entirely sure that I trust myself to drive, but I go in the middle of the day when the roads are quietest, and no harm befalls either me or my fellow drivers. When I arrive at the yard, I can't see Duke. I walk slowly around the different stables looking for him and, as far as I can see, he is nowhere in sight. Then I spot a horse that I don't recognize. He's smaller than Duke and looks in low spirits, head hanging down in a woebegone fashion. He is sad, not sleeping, as you might normally deduce from this physical stance. I look more closely.

It *is* Duke. I am torn between mentally shaking Annie and Kirsten for keeping this from me, and overwhelming relief simply at seeing him again. Later, when I mention to them how sad he looked, they say, "He missed you, Hazel." He had plenty of professional people taking care of him, but he missed me, just as I missed him. Now I really know that we are a team.

Duke doesn't hear my footfall. Perhaps my footfall has

changed over the last couple of months, as I slowly drag myself around rather than bustle here and there. So he does not look up. I call his name. It's as if he's been given an electric shock. He stands bolt upright and looks over the stable door, ears pricked, expression hopeful.

I run to him. Well, I don't really, first because I can't run at the moment, and, second, because you shouldn't run near horses; it might scare them. So I walk. But in my heart I am running. I scratch his withers, which is a whole lot nicer than a pat on the neck if you are a horse, as it's the bit on your neck that you can't reach to groom yourself. Watch two horses that are friends and they will groom each other's withers with their teeth, taking out loose hair and flaky bits of skin.

Then it begins: the ten minutes of grooming. You can't do much in ten minutes, but I reckon you can show that you care. I gently brush his back, neck, and legs, pick out his mighty hooves and do a cursory job on his tail. You could spend forty-five minutes getting the tangles out of his tail, so I'm not going to attempt it now. Then, with my physical minutes all used up, I put the grooming kit box next to him and sit there in the shadows, leaning against the stable wall, for half an hour. I tell him, quietly, how much I've missed him, how much I love him, that I am sorry he has been in pain, but relieved that he is now improving. And then I am quiet. He is quiet. He forgets that I am there and returns to the serious business of the day, eating hay, while I lean my spinning head against the stable wall and listen and watch.

Have you ever asked yourself what records you'd play on *Desert Island Discs*? It's a bit like asking yourself what you'd do if you won a million pounds. If I were lucky enough to be on *Desert Island Discs*, one track that I'd have to take would be the sound of Duke eating hay. The steady chomp-chomp-chomp slows my heart rate, and conjures scenes like this with Duke eating contentedly at the end of his day's work. To me, it is a comforting sound, rather like rain on the roof, a crackling fire, George-the-cat purring, or my mother singing. For now, this tiny amount of activity has emptied my energy tanks of everything within them. I drive home and go straight to bed, sleeping for the rest of the day. Convalescence, it would seem, cannot be rushed.

I feel as if I am standing still in thick treacle. Not only can I not move, the longer I stand still the harder moving becomes; the more something stronger than I am sucks at my legs and holds me fast. Time, for me, has not just slowed; it has stopped altogether. Bereavement is similar. So, if you've ever been bereaved, you'll know how this feels. You're walking along perfectly normally one day and the next it's as if you've run, full pelt, into a brick wall. Not only does everything hurt, but you're stunned, you can't stand up, and nothing makes sense. What I'm experiencing is, quite clearly, not as bad as bereavement, but there are similarities. Perhaps in some way I am already grieving for my father, as dementia is like a daily bereavement. Every day you lose the person that you love a little bit more. You grieve the loss of the person they were, and the losses that lie ahead.

In grief there is a feeling that your world has temporarily stopped and everyone else's is rushing on. You want to rage at people for going about their normal day-to-day lives when someone you hold dear has died. All around you people are going to work, taking children to school, talking about seemingly unimportant things, and you want to shout, "Stop! Show respect! The person I loved most in this world has died." "Stop all the clocks" indeed.

Chronic illness is similar in that everyone else's life goes on, while yours doesn't. You are a pebble in a stream that is endlessly flowing past you, never stopping. You can't join in with what they're doing. And when you're really ill, as I am now, you can't even have conversations about what they're doing, because even listening is exhausting. So there is silence.

Outside, however, the seasons are changing: a sign that, with time, my situation will change too. Nothing remains the same for ever, after all. So this must apply to my health and ability to stand up. My maternal grandmother (a true saint if ever there was one) used to say, "Good times, bad times, all times pass over," and it's true. I can see it by just looking out of the window. November can be a magical time in the woods. So, in lieu of being able to ride there, I summon up past hacks in my mind, and take them again.

I remember one when Flick and I rode out very early one November morning. We were certainly out of the yard by 8.30 a.m. This early start meant that the woods were still and untrodden when we reached them. It was rather like being the first person to walk in freshly-fallen snow. There were no dog walkers or fellow riders. For three-quarters of an hour or so, it was just us.

At the entrance to the track that goes steeply uphill into the woods from the road, the path is lined with hazel stands. At this time of year they can still be a mix of green and yellow because of their sheltered position. But within fifty yards we are soon into the deeper, golden-copper cover of the majestic beech trees, with banks of fallen leaves on either side of the treacherous chalk path. You go on like this for another 150 yards or so, under towering trees, feeling very small. Then you are presented with a choice: turn right and you loop back along the edge of fields entirely inhabited by other horses, to the fields belonging to the stables, and head quickly home. This is a ride that is so brief that you would do it only if you were extremely hard-pressed for time, your horse went lame, or you were suddenly taken ill. Even I go further than that. So our choice is to go straight on along a firm path that, even in wet weather, has only a couple of muddy stretches, so it allows us to speed up and trot.

This, if I'm honest, is my favourite bit of the whole hack, not just because we're trotting (which both Duke and I love) but because of the field maple trees. There are a handful of them towards the far end of this stretch of bridleway and in November they shine like sunlight coming in through a stained-glass window. I love beech trees. But I love the field maple more. First, the field maple (*Acer campestre*) is Britain's only native maple and, like all other maples, you can make syrup from it. So what's not to like? It is long-lived, growing up to 20 metres (60 feet) tall and can live for 350 years. It is to be found on scrubland, in woods, and, God bless it, increasingly by the side of roads, as it is tolerant of pollution.

Start looking for it as you drive along major A-roads and you'll spot it everywhere. October and November are the best time to look out for the field maple because, much as I love it, even I have to admit that most of the year its appearance is a bit boring. Its bark is light-brown, becoming a bit corky with age. It has bog-standard green leaves made of five lobes. But in autumn, to my way of thinking, the field maple outdoes all other trees. Its leaves change from green to a deep butter-yellow that is so warm and glowing that it cheers you up even on the dullest of days.

On the day that Flick and I rode out it was slightly misty and grey, a lacklustre day. Then we came to the field maples. Overnight it had been quite windy. This had blown down a great number of leaves, completely carpeting the bridleway in buttercup-yellow dry leaves. We were the first ones to reach this exquisite natural carpet and the horses trod gently over it, changing it for ever, but forming in my mind a lasting impression of beauty and joy. Now, I ride and re-ride that section in my mind, picturing the field maple leaves lifting the gloom, and they lift my spirits with them.

But this particular hack wasn't just memorable for the glorious foliage of the field maple, but because we saw a barn owl. For me, the barn owl is the most beautiful of our British owls. This is partly owing to its white plumage, but also because its silent flight makes it enigmatic and ghostly. Sadly, because of loss of habitat (for which read the industrialization of farming), their numbers have dropped by 70 per cent since the 1930s, according to the Barn Owl Trust. So, if you see one, you're very lucky. Because they are largely nocturnal, you have to know where to be and be there at night in order to see a barn owl. But in winter, they will also feed in daylight. And that was the case on this particular day. There are three owl boxes in the woods, and a mix of barn, small, and tawny owls have moved in to the new accommodation.

After the field maple delight, we'd turned right and headed down a path that is always dry whatever the weather. Because of its slight hue, we know it as the pink path. We ducked under low-hanging holly and yew branches, and skirted the spiky leaves of butcher's broom. The path takes us almost to the edge of Marwell Zoo, through mixed woodland that is in fact some of the most ancient hereabouts. We were quietly and slowly walking along this bridleway, not chatting because we were both tired so early in the morning, when a barn owl glided silently just a few feet above our heads. Barn owls have a heart-shaped face that funnels sound to their ears. So excellent is their hearing that they can detect their prey by sound alone. They can hear a mouse rustle in the leaves on the ground. This barn owl swooped gently up onto the branch of a tree about thirty feet ahead of us. It paused. Then, just as silently, it dropped out of the tree, talons outstretched, and rose up again bearing a wood mouse. It was breathtaking, and not just for the wood mouse, who sadly had breathed his last. We halted our horses and looked at one another agog. There are some things, we agreed, as we gathered our reins and walked homewards, that money can't buy. Many of them happen on horseback. And that was certainly one of them. I've only seen three barn owls in my life (though I hear the call of tawny owls from my bed during the breeding season, which runs from March to May and then again from August), and I shall never forget them. They are seared on my memory.

By the end of November, my strength has sufficiently returned to allow me to function in hour-long blocks. This means that if I enlist Flick's help in tacking Duke up, I can drive to the stables, ride him for twenty minutes, and then return home before I turn into a pumpkin. As I drive into the yard, Flick is leading Duke down the track from the woods into the stables. He is carrying a disabled man, who is clearly having a great time. I am so overwhelmed by seeing Duke again – particularly out working and obviously recovering from his lameness – that I park the car and promptly burst into tears. Flick finishes the disabled man's ride and then takes Duke up to the mounting block. I get on his back for the first time in two months. It's so wonderful simply to be back with my equine pal, as well as to be getting better, that I cry all over again. Flick, who never cries at anything, also appears to have something in her eye.

Just like Annie, all those months ago, I have to take it very steadily. Flick takes me to the outdoor arena and for twenty minutes we walk and halt repeatedly. It doesn't sound like much. That's because it isn't. But it is uplifting, encouraging, healing, fabulous, and hopeful in equal measure. If you'd told me in January that a horse would make me feel better, I'd have thought you were quite mad. Now, I take it for granted.

What I can't take for granted is that life is going to return to normal. The microbiologist's letter haunts me. Even with Phil's explanation of how things might have happened, it seems to need some fuller explanation. There is an old journalistic adage: if you don't know what you're talking about, ask someone who does. The person in this instance is the microbiologist. He does private clinics, so I separate myself from a three-figure sum and walk (very slowly) into town to see him. It is time and money well spent. But his news isn't cheery. "Well," he says, "I'd have expected you to be better by now. You must just be unlucky. It could be post-viral fatigue, in which case in a month you'll be tickety-boo." He doesn't say "tickety-boo", this not being a recognized medical term. But that's the gist of it. "Perhaps," he adds, "this is being exacerbated by something else."

So he does some more tests. I fervently hope there isn't anything else. How can there be room, with three horrid viruses living it up in my bloodstream already?

"Could it," he asks, "be HIV?" Without going into details, I explain that, er, no, it could not. "Were you," he persists, "exposed to blood on this trip?" I cast what remains of my mind back and know that, although I was exposed to bad driving, a plague of ants, damp beds, and, without a doubt, mosquitoes, I was not exposed to blood. So that's something to be grateful for.

Just when I'm starting to relax, he lands the killer blow. He explains that there are different strains of dengue fever. "If you get it a second time, you can get dengue haemorrhagic shock," he says. As I discover later, you don't recover from this. You can and will bleed to death. It's just a case of how long it will take to die horribly, frightened, far from home, and alone: a few days at the most. It may be a small risk, but it's not a risk that anyone in their right mind would wish to take. "If you're to be really safe," the microbiologist says, "this means that you can't report from countries where there is dengue fever." As there are currently more than 100 countries where dengue fever is rife, this basically means that half the world is now closed to me. And it's the half of the world where I've spent my career: developing countries in the tropics and sub-tropics.

(Years later, I will be at a conference of international journalists and we get chatting about dengue fever. One journalist from the Philippines tells me how his colleague had had the disease once, went up-country on a reporting assignment, got it again, and bled to death over seventy-two hours.)

You can get dengue fever in Singapore, the South Pacific (including the Philippines), South-East Asia, the West Indies, India, and the Middle East. But you could equally well be lying on a sun lounger in the Caribbean, or in Cuba, Central America, or the US Virgin Islands and get it. There have been cases in France. In 2009, there was an outbreak of dengue fever in the Florida town of Key West. In this particular year, there have been major outbreaks in Bolivia, Brazil, Colombia, Costa Rica, El Salvador, Honduras, Mexico, Peru, Puerto Rico, and Venezuela, as well as presumably a few people other than myself in Ethiopia. Paraguay reported a dengue outbreak so severe that hospitals were overcrowded and patients with elective surgery had to wait until the outbreak had subsided. And I've read that dengue is now the leading cause of acute febrile illness in US travellers returning from the Caribbean, South America, and Asia.

There's more bad news: "You will," the microbiologist says, "be more prone to other forms of dengue fever too now you've had this one." I look at him blankly. "What am I supposed to do?" I ask. "This is my job, my career, my passion. I love it. I get on planes and fly to troubled, underdeveloped countries. I go at the drop of a hat. I bring the stories back. I give people a voice. I tell people in the UK about those they will never meet. I can't stop doing this; it's what I do. Moreover, it's who I am."

He gives me a long, hard, Paddington-Bear stare, as if to check that I've been listening all the while. From my reaction it might appear that I haven't. He makes some suggestions: travel only in the dry season in order to reduce exposure to mosquitoes, which flourish in the wet season; check specialist health websites before travelling to see if the coast is clear; cover up from head to toe and slather yourself and your clothes in insect repellent; always stay in a room with air conditioning or an impregnated mosquito net.

What he's not saying, but doesn't need to say, is that my career, as I have known it, is over.

December

If my career as I have known it is over, I have to get back to my career. It may sound like a joke, but there must be some positives that I can rake out of this situation. If I can't get on every plane and do every story, surely there are some that I can still do without putting my health, and indeed my life, in jeopardy? It is easier, right now, to think of all the places that I can't go to rather than the ones that I can. That will change. A positive view will come. Fresh stories will be told in different countries. But it will take a few years. Neither am I well enough to be angry. Yet. That will come later too. Right now, I can't contemplate Heathrow Airport, planes, or international stories. All I want is to feel well enough to spend just a few hours at my desk.

If you've never been seriously ill this will have a hollow-laugh aspect for you. Surely, you'll be saying to yourself, the last thing that any of us really wants to be doing is sitting at our desk? What kind of an up-sucking Hermione Granger are you, anyway? The answer is that, honestly, when you haven't been able to work, you long to. I do now. So the plan is to start doing two hours of work from home in the morning and see how that goes. If it's a success, after a week I can increase it to two and a half hours, and so on. Before you know it, it will be the New Year and I'll be back working full-time.

Like all the other time-dividing plans, it works a treat, but only when I stick to it. The temptation is to go just over the two hours, or perhaps a little more, in order to get something written. This works as well as forgetting to divide my time into active, mental, and resting blocks: that is to say, not well at all. If I push myself over the two hours, the wheels fall off and I'm back on the sofa watching DVD box sets of *Spooks*. Much as I love the actor Peter Firth, who plays the lead character, Harry, I'd rather be up and living than watching him saving Britain from disaster.

So days now consist of two-hour blocks: two hours of work, two hours of rest, and two hours of something physical. I do it this way round because currently I can't quite face doing two hours of work followed by two hours of something active. But it's effective. A two-hour block is enough to go to the yard, ride, and come home again. So I decide to get back to having a few lessons. Having been away from Duke for two months, I can still remember which way to face, but my riding skills are indisputably rusty.

Flick leads Duke and me to the outdoor arena. She is grinning, which invariably means that she's got a cunning plan up her sleeve and I am about to be doing something ridiculous, like vaulting over Duke's back. It's not quite that bad, but today, she says, we will be doing the whole lesson with our reins crossed.

The aim is to stop me using my hands for every manoeuvre and to make me use my whole body in riding Duke. This is what you should be doing: using your feet, legs, bottom, hips, stomach muscles (if you have any), back, arms, shoulders, head, and neck, as well as your voice, eyes, ears, brain (again, should you have one), and attitude of mind.

I'd been relying too much on my hands and not using the rest of my body enough to communicate with Duke. While that's not the end of the world, it could be improved upon. So, swapping my reins over is intended to make me think about the rest of my body, and not my hands. It's also meant to be a bit of fun, which Flick knows that, right now, I really need. If I'm laughing about my mistakes I'm not worrying about what else is going on in my life, nor am I beating myself up about my riding errors.

She wants to show me that, even when I make mistakes, riding can still go perfectly well, or at least safely. She's trying to lift my spirits, improve my riding, and take me out of myself in half an hour. You've got to admire the girl's sense of ambition.

It is a total shambles. Duke and I go left when we want to go right and right when we mean to go left. Stopping and starting are still achievable, but everything else is a complete mess. Duke is puzzled by why I'm making such a hash of things and what on earth it is that I want him to do. All Flick and I can do is laugh. I halt Duke and lie along his dark, sweet-smelling neck, weeping with laughter. Flick never asks us to do this exercise again, but for now she has successfully taken my mind off the fact that I feel ill.

She has many inventive ways of getting me to do things. One challenge is to keep my leg on the horse at all times. I'm forever taking it off and giving a little kick instead of keeping my leg nice and still on Duke's side. Why does this matter? Well, no one likes to be kicked, do they? It's not what you'd class as encouragement. But leaving your leg on the horse's side tells him that you want him to keep going. It's a bit like keeping your foot in a steady position on the accelerator pedal in your car. Once you're driving along a motorway, you can hopefully just leave it in a set position unless you need to brake. But because I forget to do this, Flick asks me to imagine that I've got a £50 note lodged between each calf muscle and Duke's stomach. If I move my legs, those beautiful red notes are going to fly off in the breeze, never to be seen again. That certainly focuses the mind, though we don't do it for real, as neither of us has two £5 notes to spare, let alone two £50s.

Another trick is carrying my hands level. Why does this matter? Because my hands are attached to Duke's mouth, through the reins and the bit. So any pulling or uneven use of my hands can be felt in his mouth. Unpleasant. The aim, therefore, is to keep my hands still and level, not emphasizing one or the other. But I am right-handed and invariably overuse my right hand when riding, for just about anything: halting, turning, attempting to open gates, bending. You name it, I do too much of it with my right hand.

Worse, when I panic or am frightened, I lift my right hand up. I don't mean to. It's an involuntary habit that we need to break, as it puts a stress on the right-hand side of Duke's mouth, and thus is something we want to avoid at all costs. So Flick gives me a small riding crop and asks me to hold it level between my hands whilst also holding the reins and riding. This is fantastically difficult at first, but is brilliant, because I can see when my right hand is rising up, pulling back, opening out in a non-level way from the left hand. Holding the riding crop keeps my hands more level than they usually are, so we are all happy.

Then there's my posture. The best riders look as though, if you took the horse away, they'd just be standing on the ground with their knees bent. Their heads are held high. They are looking ahead. Their shoulders are back. Their legs drop straight down the horse's sides with only a tiny bend in the knee, and their feet are flat, horizontal with the ground. This position gives you the greatest control. You can go any speed and stop like this. Furthermore, if you stay like this, you are unlikely to fall off because you are beautifully balanced.

I'd like to look like this, but I don't. I look as if I'm sitting on a sofa holding a book. Even if I remember to hold my head up, look straight ahead, put my shoulders back, and keep my hands level, my legs are never, ever straight. There is, I think, no hope. But Flick is determined that we should try to improve my posture. So every session starts with five or ten minutes of mounted exercise. Depending on her mood, this can be at any speed: walk, trot, or canter (though if it's canter, it'll be on another horse, so I can see that particular moment of doom approaching as soon as I arrive at the yard). Flick puts Duke, let's say, on a lunge line, working him from the centre of a circle. I tie up my reins and lift my stirrups over his back. Yes, folks, you've got that right: I have nothing to put my feet on and nothing to hold on to. This is core muscle exercise for toughies. Forget doing The Plank in the gym: ride a horse with no stirrups and reins and you will develop stomach muscles.

Then off we go, first in walk, then in trot, and all the time Flick's shouting commands: "Put your hands on your head; now out to the sides; now up in the air; now in front of you. Now circle your arms forwards, and back. Turn your body to the left, now to the right, and again, and again. Pat your stomach. Keep your head up. Once again from the beginning. Remember to breathe…"

It's fantastic. It works. But it is initially terrifying. Wobble just ever so slightly and you're off. The point, of course, is not to wobble. Thankfully, Flick makes some concessions to my age. The children who learn here get much harder tasks, all dressed up as fun. They have to go "around the world" on the horse: first facing forward, then sitting facing to the right on the saddle, then moving round facing the rear, then facing the left, then back to the front. They do this with the horse standing still, but they do it with the horse moving too. She is breeding trick riders, I'm convinced.

The toughest exercise I've seen Flick give anyone is to carry two full mugs of water whilst riding. One of her other pupils, an eleven-year-old girl, is clearly destined for great things in the equine world. She is über-talented and wins everything she enters. It helps that she has a fabulously supportive mum and her own pony, but still, the child can ride. Flick is teaching her the hands-level-and-still trick. Only, with this little girl, Lauren, she does not use a short riding crop; she sends for two mugs of cold water. Lauren has to ride whilst holding one in each hand, keeping her elbows tight into her sides, not moving her legs, looking ahead and, yes, making her pony keep going. At first, there are complaints about how much it hurts. But then she gets good at it. She's walking, trotting, and ultimately cantering round the outdoor arena, carrying two mugs of water whilst riding a pony. It's extraordinary. I hope Flick will never ask me to do this, as I won't do it as well. Furthermore, I'll spill all the water and be soaked to the skin.

Phil says, "You've been doing this for a while. Haven't you learned to ride yet?" I try to explain that – for me, at least – learning to ride is not like learning to read. It's taking longer. In fact, in my own defence, all the great riders go on having lessons to improve what they are doing. And if it's good enough for international competitors, it's good enough for me. He looks doubtful. Perhaps I am, he suggests, just spending money?

Whatever I'm doing financially, I am on a drive to improve my health however I can. As well as riding, I'm eating local, seasonal foods, sourced from Winchester's fabulous, bi-monthly farmers' market. Eating this way means that I'm getting the greatest amount of nutrients from my fruit and vegetables, as they haven't travelled far and are thus fresh. I opt for meat either from my chums at Hampshire Game or from Hyden Farm, a wonderful family-run farm that specializes in organically reared rare breeds. I've eaten in some swanky restaurants in my time, but, to my mind, it's impossible to beat the quality of the meat that these two companies provide.

Eating well isn't enough. My immune system requires a bit of help. Clare reminds me that a few years ago when I had meningitis (or was it tick-borne encephalitis?), it was acupuncture that helped me to recover. "Why don't you try that again?" she says. Up to now, it hasn't been an option. A session with Karen Erskine, the local acupuncturist, takes an hour, and I have to walk there and back. But now that I'm into two-hour time slots, I can manage this. I ring Karen. She magically creates an appointment for me in her busy schedule and, before I know it, I'm lying on her treatment bed having needles stuck into me.

Acupuncture is a complete medical system from China that dates back 3,000 years and is used to treat anything from headaches to heart attacks. Its purpose is to treat the root cause of those headaches and heart attacks (and everything in between) by plugging into so-called energy lines that run through the body. Along these energy lines are many acupuncture points, which have specific functions to treat particular illnesses or problems.

Karen holds my wrists to feel my pulses. She's listening not only to my heart rate but also for the quality of that heart rate, which can tell her if I'm stressed or exhausted and how all my internal organs (not just my heart) are functioning. She looks grave. "Your tank is only 10 per cent full," she says. "We've got to build up your immune system before you can do anything much. If you overdo it now, your tank will never refill. Once we've got you up to about 50 per cent, then you can start doing things: not before."

So it begins: weekly sessions of being turned into a human pin cushion. But other than Duke, this is the only thing that helps. I feel that, slowly, my strength is returning. It matters not one jot that I don't fully understand how acupuncture works. All that matters is that I'm feeling better. Sceptics would say, "Ah, that's the placebo effect." Even if it is that, I welcome it. Having enough energy to get through a normal day is all I want. If acupuncture helps, then I will happily have needles stuck into me for an hour every week.

With time on my hands still, ironically, I am able to prepare for the perfect Christmas: the one I didn't have last year. I am able to order the meat, plan the menu, and buy and send presents and cards early. Of course, the perfect Christmas, which I'd mocked a year ago, requires more than simply being organized. It requires you to be happy, healthy, and with those you love. Ah: three major stumbling blocks there, then.

In the run-up to Christmas, I visit Daddy. He talks, as he always does, about coming home. When can he come? He could stay at my house if he can't go back to his own house, he suggests. It needs to happen soon. He has, as ever, packed a variety of his things into his dirty linen basket, in lieu of a suitcase. While we are chatting, I quietly put them away again. He does this a lot and his choice is always random: photographs, shoes, a couple of jumpers, his book of British birds, and sometimes even a pot plant.

It's poignant, heartbreaking stuff. He feels dumped here. Equally, I feel that I have dumped him. If I had a vast private income and could afford to pay a live-in member of staff, I could then possibly bring him home. But I can't bring a confused, ailing man back to my house and then go to work, or even just try to continue to get well. It's a misery. I sit and hold his hands and explain, once again, that I am dreadfully sorry, but he can't come home. No matter how much we would love it to be thus, it won't be. Ever. He's not going to get any better. His needs are now such that expert care is the best thing for him. Mummy and I wouldn't do such a good job. We couldn't cope. That would be worse for him and ultimately, therefore, for us too. I've seldom seen him cry and can remember only a couple of times from my childhood. The first time I was too young to know what it was about. The second time, his cat Paddy had died… He holds my hands and silently weeps. I cry too. This is a moment of clarity in the encircling gloom of dementia, a moment when he understands just how awful this illness is.

We talk about it and he says that, frankly, he'd much rather have had a heart attack like his father, or a stroke like his mother, and died quickly. This, he says, is not what he wanted, not what he wants now. But there is no way out. Decades earlier, both he and my mother had written living wills. These are documents that set out a person's desire regarding future medical treatment in circumstances in which they are unable to give informed consent. Like now, for instance. My mother and I turn their house upside down looking for these documents. We can't find them. We ring the family solicitor to see if he's got them. He hasn't. Somewhere along the line, probably during a house move, these precious documents have gone astray. And, as they were done so long ago, even my mother can't remember what was in them. Did the wishes apply to withholding treatment only if they had a heart attack, or also if they were in a car accident that resulted in brain damage, meaning they would have no quality of life? Was dementia even mentioned? Was dementia on anyone's radar back then? Ironically, no one can remember. All I can recall is that these documents were once drawn up. So my father had a desire not to linger in a half-world. Now, that desire can't be honoured.

And, if it could, what would we do, exactly? He is not on a life-support system, so we couldn't withdraw that. The options would be to stop giving him food and water and kill him slowly, or, somehow, kill him quickly. This is, of course, completely unthinkable. I love my father. I cannot kill him, or see him be killed. The thought is monstrous. But he doesn't want to live like this. We don't want him to live like this. But what is certain is that he is going to go on living like this, slowly fading, until the day he dies, which nobody wants, least of all him.

I do not believe in euthanasia. Life is precious, after all. We are not God; these are not our choices. But this amount of daily suffering challenges that belief. I rage at the dementia, longing for it to end but knowing that, the day it does, my father will no longer be alive. The end of the dementia means never being able to talk to my dad again about life, birds, cats, plants, God, or cricket. There are no good outcomes in this scenario. There will not be, as the church has it, a good death.

Over the last few years I've learned not to talk about this. It's too personal, precious, and awful to discuss with anyone. And, generally, most people cling to the fiction that my father is going to get better, or have good days, or somehow be happy in his infirmity. All this is tosh, born of an understandable desire not to look the horror in the eyes. So I haven't talked about it. But sometimes now I do. Then I always regret it, because unless you've walked this particular path, it is hard to understand how you could wish that your beloved parent would die. "Life is God-given," one friend tells me sternly. "We should fight for every breath." "Yes," I say; "I agree. But this isn't life; this is merely existing. How do we feel about that, exactly?"

Lest you think I am a dreadful hypocrite, let me say at this point that my father's dementia has made me seriously consider what I would want to happen if I were to be struck down by this illness. Getting dementia is now my greatest fear; I have nightmares about it. Phil reassures me that it isn't hereditary. But I know that, as we are all living longer, the chance of succumbing to dementia is increasing. There are no wars or plagues to kill us all off young. That's a good thing, of course. But losing your wits isn't an excellent corollary. So I sit Phil down and explain that, should the day come when I have dementia and I am no longer able to cope alone, I want him to take me outside to the garden bench one cold, frosty night and leave me there. In the morning I'll have died of cold. It'll be better all round. Suffice it to say that this does not go down well with someone who's made a pledge to save lives.

Sitting with your father, crying, as he realizes that he's never going to get better or come home, and then facing what you'd do under the same circumstances, are not cheerful Advent occupations. But possibly we dress up Christmas into something it isn't. Mary looking serene in a blue gown, holding a healthy, clean child, while Joseph and the animals look on in wonder. Nonsense. What about the long journey a young, heavily pregnant woman made to a town far from home, where she knew no one? How about the rejection that the couple would have faced when they got there? They weren't married yet and she was pregnant. That may be perfectly normal today, but back in first-century Palestine you could get stoned to death for it.

Then imagine having nowhere to stay. Either people won't let you in because you lower the tone, or the whole place is crammed, or both. And so you end up giving birth to your first child, as I've mentioned, in a stable full of all sorts of animals. There is blood, poo, pain, and screaming. And, in the midst of all this, you're wondering if you heard God right. What on earth is going on? How can you be pregnant? What is this going to do to your relationship with Joseph, your future husband; your family; your friends? Talk about terrifying.

So what I'm contemplating is a real Christmas, not a fake one. My Christmas, like the original one, is full of pain, questions, and difficulties, but also peace and hope. But before all that there is still some Christmas shopping to be done. Phil decides that two brains are better than one when it comes to present shopping, even if one of those brains is mine. We walk into town to join the milling throng out on a last-minute gift hunt. I know it's not going to work out well as soon as we get into the first shop: my head is already spinning and I feel light-headed with exhaustion. We visit two more shops. After this, I bail out and somehow walk back up the long hill to home alone, leaving Phil to contend with the crowds and his credit card. I go to bed and sleep for two and a half hours. I'm not yet as strong as I had thought.

This is confirmed the next day, when, having made a wreath for the front door, put up the Christmas tree, and done what amounts to my regular food shop at the farmers' market, I keel over once again and head for the sofa. But part of the challenge of recovery is to think about what I can do, rather than what I can't. It's about thinking positively: believing in hope, health, and better times, even if they are not yet upon me.

At the stables, Flick is saying something similar about riding. "Look at what you've achieved this year," she says. "At the start of the year you were a tiny, terrified rider on the back of a big horse. But things have changed, haven't they? Now you and Duke are a partnership. Now no one thinks of you as a nervous rider; you just stand out because you're so small and he's so big. Everyone here, and all along the road, knows you and you know everyone else. That's built your confidence, hasn't it?"

Indeed it has. In the days to come, people out running, riding, or walking dogs along Hensting Lane will still stop me and ask how Duke is, remembering the quirky combination of petite rider and thumping great big horse. Quietly, as if through a side door, I've joined an outdoor world, made new friends, and, crucially, found a motivation in life that isn't a copy deadline. It is enormously refreshing.

Keith, one of my journalist pals, laughs at me and says, "Now, for you, the answer to every question is 'horse riding'." It's true. Think of the questions:How do you spend your money? What do you enjoy doing in your spare time? What would you much rather be doing right now? What makes you come alive? If there were only one thing left in your life, what would it be?

It's a remarkable transition. A year ago, I wouldn't have been able to answer those questions. True, I spent far too much money on shoes and ball gowns. But I didn't have much spare time in which to wear them. There were no holidays. The only thing that made me come alive was finding a story and seeing it published in a national newspaper. And reporting was the only thing in my life other than my faith and friends. What a difference a year makes.

We edge up to Christmas uncertain what it will bring. It will be different from previous festive seasons, but how will that affect us all? It has been decided that the best thing is for my father to stay in the care home over Christmas. We will visit on Boxing Day. He doesn't take this well, to the point where my mother has a sit-down discussion with the care home's manager about whether or not we could or should bring him home. "No," she says gently, "that wouldn't be wise. He needs to settle, and if he returns home that will only take longer."

Old traditions forged over forty years are instantly abandoned. New festive traditions have to be made. The first is to drive to Hyden Farm to collect the meat. The farm lies in the depths of the South Downs and is reached down a long, narrow lane. There are many ways to get there. I say this because I have never used the same route and always, always get lost. This year is no exception. We get lost repeatedly. But instead of finding that stressful or tense, we laugh at my stupidity. We stop at the famous Bat and Ball pub in Hambledon – the village that is the original home of cricket – and have lunch. Mummy describes the whole fiasco as "a treat", revealing her good will, that mistakes aren't to be taken too seriously, and that a new tradition has been born.

On Christmas Eve, Phil and I visit my father, bearing a hamper of tasty goodies. He seems genuinely pleased, though weeks later I'll discover everything forgotten and consequently uneaten and mouldy. It will all have to be thrown away. But for now, in this moment, he enjoys it, eating a few chocolates and a slice of cake. I'd been dreading this, but Phil's diverting presence changes the dynamic and it all passes off smoothly.

Christmas Day itself comes and goes in a flurry of cooking, eating, and present giving, until we haul ourselves out of the warmth of the dining room, away from the wood-burning stove, and down to Winchester Cathedral for evensong. The fading afternoon light slants through the stained-glass windows. It is a liminal time of day. Candles are lit. The choir processes. The Christmas tree lights the west end of the nave. It is ethereal and lifts me beyond myself, beyond this year, up towards something profound. If God reaches out to us, through his Son, at this bleak time of the year, then we are not alone in our troubles. I am not alone. It may have been dreadful. It may still be dreadful, and it is. But I am not in it by myself. There is a flicker of light in the darkness.

On Boxing Day, we visit Daddy. Initially, he is furious. He says that everyone – including us, obviously – "hates" him, as he had no company yesterday. It's a grim beginning. But I remind him that we visited on Christmas Eve and here we are again today, and that we do love him very much. He looks bemused. Part of the tragedy of this stage of dementia is that, because your short-term memory is shot to bits, you can't remember when you've seen people, so you feel very lonely. Five minutes after we've left, it will be as if we were never there. And it's the never-there bit that he latches on to. There is nothing to be done but make the best of the moment we are in. So we do, with tea, cake, and light, gentle chat, as much of it as possible about Christmases that my father can remember, when he was a child.

In January, I will return to reporting, and time will do its healing work for all of us: strengthening my mother; giving me a fresh focus; settling my father into this, his final home. But,for now, there are a few days before New Year in which I can do as I please. And what I please is to be with Duke. Friends visit from America. We all head to the yard. The children have a riding lesson with Flick in the outdoor arena. I take myself off and quietly tack Duke up. Then I ride and they all walk, round the woods, as I am keen to show off my new world, my new little bit of paradise. Despite thick mud, they love it. My chum Jim is a long-established horse rider and, though he generally prefers a horse with go-faster stripes, he is looking admiringly at Duke. I dismount and hand him my hard hat and the horse, and he trots off through the woods, beaming. We catch up with him ten minutes later. He and Duke are waiting at the far end of the woods at the top of the steep track, quietly, calmly. Duke with ears pricked. "He's a nice horse," says Jim. "That's an understatement," I say.

On New Year's Eve, Annie, Kirsten, and I join two others on a big end-of-year hack. We ride through the woods, past Marwell Zoo, and up to a lovely local pub and back. Once out in the fields alongside Marwell, Duke is so delighted that he puts on a real turn of speed and enthusiasm. Unusually, I have to ask everyone else if they mind speeding up a bit, as he is keen to get on. Normally I'm asking people to slow down. But not today. Duke is happy, loving being taken out of normal duties and allowed out round Hampshire's beautiful countryside doing ordinary horse-like things. I'm happy because he's happy. We are, it dawns on me, a team.

Our last time along this route was inauspicious as Duke circumvented primroses and dived off sideways at a canter into the crops to get away from the ostriches. Not this time. He is unfazed by giraffe, deer, and even the dreaded ostriches. I am not waiting for anything to go wrong. I believe in him. I believe in myself. We are trotting through the field grinning. We are both, unexpectedly, happy.

The woods are quieter than usual on New Year's Eve. There are no runners, cyclists, or even other horse riders. Once through the long field we stroll steadily back through the woods, weaving our way through the hazel stands and beech trees, spotting roe deer in a field to our right, and endlessly walking over a carpet of brown-gold beech leaves.

We return to the yard muddy, sweaty, and exhilarated. It has been a fitting end to a life-changing year. As I lie in bed that night, eschewing parties and fireworks, I look back over the past twelve months. Overall, I'm surprised to realize that it's been a good year. Yes, it has been fraught with emotional pain and physical illness. But that is not what I remember as I reflect on the year that is slipping away. I remember a large, dark horse; the woods; and a growing sense that anything is possible with love. Tomorrow, as I wake to face the next year, I will not groan. There will be a reason to smile and a reason to get up in the morning, and that reason is Duke.

What Happened Next

Five years have passed since I first set eyes on Duke. It is now hard to imagine what my life was like before him. What did I do with my hard-earned cash? How did I spend my weekends? What did I do on summer evenings? The answers are: wasted it; ran around doing an endless list of chores; went to aerobics classes. You can see that my life has been materially improved by the presence of a horse who is now on the cusp of retirement.

What's been interesting about these five years is that I've spent them doing something that I don't naturally excel at. This is very rare. Ask yourself, when does this happen in your life? I'll wager that it doesn't. It's certainly never happened before in my life. Think about it: once you get to secondary school, life is all about whittling out the subjects that are the equivalent of Serbo-Croat to you and focusing on the things that you enjoy and do well. That goes on until you're eighteen. Then you narrow it down again, picking the degree course, further education study, or apprenticeship that is your strongest suit. After that, you choose your career. Whether you're a plumber, a politician, or a tree surgeon, you end up specializing, often again and again, until you find your niche in life.

I love being a reporter. It's so much fun getting out and about asking people questions and then writing the story. It is, truly, the best job in the world and I like to think that I'm good at it. I feel that I'm a messenger between the person I'm meeting and the reader. That's true whether it's an asylum seeker in Austria, a Romani gypsy child in Serbia, a smart hotelier in France, or a farmer in Britain. But earlier in my career I kept being overpromoted, made editor of this-and-that, because that was the next step up and I seemed like a reasonable candidate. But I soon learned that if I wasn't outside tramping the streets, asking people questions, I was as miserable as a caged lion, or perhaps that should be a lioness. Editing looked more prestigious and was, but it wasn't my forte. Indoors, I growled a lot. I was good, it turned out, at being a hack. So I returned to it, writing for newspapers and magazines, as well as for various charitable organizations.

In my spare time, such as it was, I did other things that I was reasonably good at: aerobics, dancing, and lots of cooking – I simply adored inviting people round for meals and did so several times a week. So there wasn't any space for doing something that I didn't seem to be good at. Duke created that space. Let's face it: I was a rubbish rider to start off with. In fact, I was rubbish for quite a long time. Partly, this was because I believed I was dreadful. I believed that other people were riders and I wasn't. I thought that I didn't belong in the horse-riding world; I was a fraud. Sometimes, not surprisingly, others viewed me like this too.

So I could have gone on for ever thinking that I didn't belong in the saddle. I compared myself with others: people who'd been riding since childhood; astonishingly gung-ho riders who loved nothing more than blasting across the countryside at full speed; gifted dressage riders, and even, in the case of eleven-year-old Lauren, talented children. But comparisons are odious, as my grandmother and mother always said.

In time, with the help of Duke, Flick, and my riding buddies who were indefatigably positive and encouraging, I rewrote the script. I stopped believing that I was useless and started to believe that I could ride. So I did ride and I enjoyed it. I became unfazed by farm vehicles in the road, opening gates, even the effects of primroses and sabre-toothed pigeons. There were caveats to this belief, of course. I prefer riding Duke to other horses. If I'm honest, I only want to ride him. I know him. I love being with him. There are fewer surprises than when I ride a different horse. But I have ridden other horses.

The most memorable occasion was on the Isles of Scilly, where I rode with a young instructor. We rode down to a deserted beach and then out to the far-off tide, our horses standing and dozing with their feet in a few inches of seawater. It was such a blissful experience that it reduced me to tears of joy. I've ridden my friend Kirsty Hobson's horse, Spider, who looked after me and improved what was a very tough day. More of that anon. But I avoid riding fast, unpredictable horses that I don't know. The deep heart of my fear is still there, though it may be greatly reduced in size. Also, I prefer to ride in the company of others. Duke does too. We are both more relaxed then, so where is the shame in admitting it and simply enjoying gentle rides? As I've gone on, I've realized that many people feel just the same. I am not an outsider any more. I can ride at my own, admittedly reasonably low, level, and I love it. I won't be giving any professional riders a run for their money, but presumably they won't be offering to write a national newspaper feature in a couple of hours either.

Confidence also came simply through looking after Duke. In fact, this has been the biggest pleasure. I can spend any amount of time in Duke's stable, grooming him. Now, I've spent five years with Duke, listening to him, and so remarkably I know as much about him and his needs as anyone. That's a big change from not knowing how to pick out his hooves.

Listening, of course, is the journalist's core skill. You listen not just to what people say, but crucially also to what they *don't* say. You listen for the nuances, the inferences, the hidden meanings.

You wait, quietly, for them to say the thing (whatever it is) that they've been longing to tell someone, but never dared. You need the facts, but you listen to the emotions. You watch how people say things and their body language as they speak – or don't, as the case may be. It is absolutely no use trying to lie to me. I will sniff out a lie at twenty paces. I know a fraud when I see one. And so does Duke.

Horses take you as you are. So you have to learn to put down your emotions at the stable door. That was a challenge during this particular year, when my whole body vibrated with emotions, most of them negative. He listened to me, and reflected my emotions back to me. If I was shaking with anger, he would put his ears back, a sure sign that he did not welcome me or my emotions. If I was calm and relaxed, he'd put his enormous head in my arms and doze off.

In doing this, he taught me to try to be calmer than I felt: hence the singing in Latin. But decades of reporting made me able to listen to him in return. It is said that a good rider can hear his horse speak, but that a really good one can hear him whisper. I will never be the most technically competent, or confident, rider. But I can hear Duke whisper. I listened as he told me, through body language, about mites, scabs, a reaction to mud, and – endlessly – the almost comic requirement for more long grass. So, with the help of the yard's experienced team, including Flick and Tracey, he has no mites, no scabs, and no mud fever (though as I write it is getting muddy outside because of endless rain), but there is always the desire for long grass.

He let it be known that he loves to ride through the woods with one other horse. Big hacks with lots of riders he eschews. They go too fast for him and keeping up can become stressful. A gentle stroll with one other pal is right up Duke's street. Jack, a twelve-year-old Welsh Section C pony, is his favourite hacking companion. He pricks his ears when he hears Jack and Debbie coming down the road, and then lowers his mighty head and greets Jack. He's made it clear that he prefers hay to haylage, thanks very much, and that, as a treat, I should feel welcome to bring him a Garlic Likit: the equivalent of a lollipop for horses. Of course, I do.

We have spent as much of the five intervening years in the woods as we could. I think we'd both like to go more often, but we both have other duties. Life cannot be all beech leaves and hazel stands. We've done a few dressage competitions and even been to a show. Not *The Sound of Music*; this is a show where you present your horse in a glowing state of health and run alongside him as he walks and trots. Yes, that really is the way that some people spend their weekend. He loved that. We have a very funny picture of him trotting, at a considerable lick, with me trying to keep up alongside. There are no prizes for guessing that because of this we didn't win, but it was a lark.

We've also spent a fair amount of time avoiding torrential rain, hail, snow, ice, pheasant shoots, high winds, and fireworks: sometimes several of them at the same time. This has meant staying in a warm stable with both of us eating apples. We've stood gazing at the purple-blue glory of carpets of bluebells, and watched the autumn leaves fall; and we know where that patch of primroses is now. Mercifully, the ostriches have moved. We have seen the seasons change together. As we've done this, I've felt more whole and closer to God than I often do in church.

It's not just me that's happy. "Duke," someone told me the other day, "is a different horse when he's with you. He loves you." And it is true to say that, whenever he sees me coming, he strolls across his field, puts his mighty head down so that I can reach up to put his head collar on, and follows me as if to say, "What are we doing today, and can I have some long grass on the way, please?"

I have asked if I can buy him more times than the founder of the yard can stand. She loves him too, knowing a good horse when she sees one, and wants to keep him for ever. You can understand that, can't you? I can, and I respect her decision. But everyone needs a dream, even if it won't come true. The reality of owning Duke, of course, would involve early mornings, late nights, vet's bills, farrier's bills, poo, wee, and a lot of time. It would be messy. It would be an adventure. But it might take more time, strength, money, and knowledge than I currently have. The dream is lovely, but in reality I'm very lucky simply to have Duke on loan. We have a pretty idyllic situation. I get all the fun, without the 5 a.m. starts and the bills for hay, medicine, and shoes. If I am sent on a foreign assignment, I know that the team at Hampshire Riding Therapy Centre will love and look after Duke until I return. So I'll keep on riding Duke for as long as they allow me to and as long as he lives, because to do so gives me the greatest joy. I'll sit in the stable, feed him apples, take care of his legs, and thank God for the day that I met him, because being with him is the highlight of my life.

The truth is that Duke got me through not only this particular year, but all five of them. It is hard to envisage how I would have managed without him. My father's condition slowly deteriorated, as you would expect. He forgot where he had lived, so stopped asking to go back there. He soon forgot my name, or who I was. But he still knew that I was someone he loved. Towards the end, I asked him one day if he could remember who I was. "Not really," he said. "But you are lovely and full of smiles."

"That," said Phil, "is the kind of testimony we would all like." He forgot the happy years that he'd spent with the RAF. He forgot the name of his wife of forty-something years. He forgot the name of the village where he had grown up, played football, and picked cherries.

Then his body started to forget how to do things. Soon he couldn't stand or walk unaided. He became doubly incontinent, but lost the power of speech and the vocabulary that would have enabled him to ask to go to the toilet. He lost his dignity and virtually everything that had made him the person he had been. But, oddly, he didn't forget that he was a life-long *Guardian* reader. In the year before his death in 2014, one day I had a big feature in *The Daily Telegraph*. He'd always disliked *The Telegraph* (though not quite as much as the *Daily Mail*) for its right-wing politics. He'd taken *The Guardian* for most of his adult life and nothing would sway him from it. Nonetheless, I thought the feature would give me something to talk about when I visited him. His face lit up when he saw the picture of me in the feature, but then he looked at me quizzically. "I know," I said jokingly, "it's *The Telegraph*. You know how you love *The Telegraph*."

"Not so much," he said. Some things, it seems, never fade.

On 28 December 2014 I was sitting in front of a roaring fire with George-the-cat, about to watch *Antiques Roadshow*. (How middle-aged is that?) Then the phone rang. It was the duty manager at the care home. "Your father is very ill," she said. "His cough has gone to his chest and now his breathing sounds laboured. You should come."

Just like the moment when my mother had her stroke, everything froze. "Come now?" I asked, trying to establish what she was really saying. "Or in the morning?"

"Now," she said.

I drove to my mother's house and we went together. The streets were deserted on this cold, frosty, starlit night. We drove in near-silence to the care home to say our goodbyes. He was already unconscious, but we said them anyway: prayed, read his favourite Bible verses, held his hand, stroked his hair, wept, and thanked him for the fun times. He died at 6 a.m. the next day. I thought that I had no more grief left in me, having grieved for him every day of the ten years that he had lived with dementia. But I did.

My father's funeral took place in a beautiful woodland burial site in Hampshire a few weeks later. He's buried under beech trees and was taken to his grave by my friends Ness and Charlotte in an historic reed-gathering wagon pulled by two Suffolk Punch horses. Afterwards, over cups of tea, everyone said how beautiful the wood was and how they'd loved the horses – even friends and relatives who live in London and wouldn't look at a horse if you paid them.

The day after the funeral, my friend Kirsty rang me and told me to get to her yard promptly: I needed to ride off the tears, she said. I disagreed, but went anyway. She let me ride her horse Spider, and we whizzed along country lanes, galloped through the woods, and squealed with excitement as the mud and leaves flew. It was a tonic, and one that, eight years ago, I would never have considered.

My mother recovered from her stroke and the stress of my father's illness. She lives brightly, positively, and radiantly, not knowing that she is a joy to everyone who meets her. At the age of eighty-eight, she's still having new experiences, going on a canal boat for the first time last summer (2015) and loving it.

Back at the stables, horses have come and gone. Annie bought Lady. Debbie bought Jack. Kirsten decided to ride a friend's horse, and Kirsty has bought so many horses that she could start her own polo team. But she prefers charging across the New Forest at speed. Duke and I continue to stroll round the woods. We may be an unlikely partnership, but we are a happy one.

Postscript

Duke died on 15 February 2016.

He was much loved and will never be forgotten.